W9-BKH-729

The Reunion Planner

The Step-by-Step Guide Designed to Make Your
Reunion a Social and Financial Success!

Linda Johnson Hoffman
and
Neal Barnett

Goodman Lauren Publishing
Los Angeles, California

Goodman Lauren Publishing
11661 San Vicente Blvd. Suite 505
Los Angeles, CA 90049

This book is designed to provide information in regard to the subject matter contained herein. While every effort has been made to provide complete and accurate information, the authors and publisher assume no responsibility for errors or omissions. Neither is any liability assumed for damages resulting from the use of the information contained herein.

Front and back covers designed by Mark Luscombe

Illustrations by Elizabeth Aldridge Holmes

Library of Congress Catalog Card Number: 91-73738

Publisher's Cataloging in Publication
(Prepared by Quality Books Inc.)

Hoffman, Linda Johnson,
    The reunion planner: the step-by-step guide designed to make your reunion a social and financial success / Linda Johnson Hoffman and Neal Barnett.
    p. cm.
    Includes bibliographical references and index.
    ISBN 0-9630516-2-8
    1. Class reunions--Planning. 2.Reunions--Planning. I. Barnett, Neal. II. Title. III. Title: The step-by-step guide designed to make your reunion a social and financial success.

LB3618.H6 1992   793.2379
                                     QBI92-10607

First Printing 1992

10 9 8 7 6 5 4 3 2 1

This book is dedicated to
the memory of Mari Sedny

Contents

Preface   ix

Acknowledgements   xi

Introduction   1
What This Book Offers You   1
Professional Reunion Planners   4
Making the Decision to Plan Your Reunion   7
Getting the Most Value From This Book   8
How This Book is Structured   11
Overview   12

GETTING ORGANIZED

1   **Twelve Months Before the Reunion**   15
The Groundwork in Three Steps   15
Step 1. Make Key Contacts   15
Step 2. Search For Alumni   20
*Step 3. Decide When and Where to
           Have the Reunion*   24

Reunion Checklist   31

2	**The Budget**	35
	Assumptions	36
	Estimated Expenses	39
	Estimated Revenues	41
	Estimated Balance	43
	The Computer Program's Budget Report	44

THE FOOTWORK

3	**How To Increase Attendance**	47
	Portray an Enticing Reunion	47
	Dealing with Reluctant Reunion Attendees	50
	"You'll Wonder Why You Even Hesitated"	54

4	**Nine Months Before the Reunion**	57
	Prepare the First Mailing	57
	Provide Entertainment	63
	Hire the Photographer	66
	Plan the Picnic	67
	Set up a Bank Account	68

5	**Six Months Before the Reunion**	69
	The Memory Album	69
	Name Tags	71
	The Second Mailing	73
	Tickets and Acknowledgements	76

6	**Three Months Before the Reunion**	79
	The Phone Drive	79
	Media Announcements	81
	Decorations, Displays and Other Mementos	81
	Reception Desk Workers	85

THE COUNTDOWN

7 One Month Before the Reunion 89
Reminder Notices 89
Make Name Tags 89
The Program 90
Door Prizes and Awards 94
Set up the Decorations 95
Photographer Cards 96

8 Two Weeks Before the Reunion 97
The Attendance List 97
Loose Ends 98
Mail the Tickets 99

9 One Week Before the Reunion 101
Registration 101
*Final Arrangements with the Facility
    or Caterer* 105
Contingency Plan 106

REUNION DAY AND AFTERWARDS

10 The Reunion Event 109
At Home 109
At the Facility 111
The Reunion 112
Before Leaving the Event 113
The Picnic 113

11 After the Reunion 115
Closing Costs and Responsibilities 115
Concluding Comments 118

POSTSCRIPT

Meeting A Challenge in Locating People   121

Survey   125

APPENDICES

A   **Sample Invitations**   131

B   **Sample Questionnaire/Survey**   135

C   **Sample Accounting Ledgers**   137

        Bibliography   141

        Index   143

Preface

In my professional career, I have participated in the planning of many large entertainment events, political campaign dinners, fund raisers and charity functions. That is why it seemed so natural for me to initiate the planning of my ten, twenty and twenty-five year high school reunions.

Following the successful completion of my twenty-year high school reunion, I was encouraged by Neal Barnett, a friend and systems analyst, to collaborate on a reunion planning package. This would consist of a guidebook and computer program to describe and simplify reunion planning. His idea was intriguing. Reunions are taking place every year and since we could find no such package or computer program in the marketplace, we decided that such a product was definitely needed.

With my experience at planning reunions, I would write the book, and with Neal's computer programming skills, he would design a software program. Four years later, having completed our respective tasks, while at the same time supplementing each other's main expertise, we produced this book and the computer program in the hope that reunion committees will greatly benefit from this package.

Planning a reunion is a unique and gratifying experience, but also time consuming in today's busy lifestyle. However, planning is the essence of success in this effort. This reunion guide gives confidence to you, the planners, while streamlining your efforts toward this infrequent and very special occasion.

Good luck and have a great reunion.

Acknowledgements

This book not only involved every spare moment Neal and I could capture in the last four years, it also represents the contributions of many people, including family and some very dear friends.

The illustrations contained in this book represent the hard work and charming nature of Elizabeth Aldridge Holmes. Her pictures brought levity and personality to this reunion guide. The front and back cover designs were created by Mark Luscombe. Mark not only provided distinctive creativity, but his assistance on the book production process also was helpful. Thank you both for all your efforts.

I would like to express deepest gratitude for my friend, Mari Sedny, who spent many hours on the initial editing process of this manuscript. Final editing contributions were provided by Marlene Vallen. Their writing skills and expertise lent clarity and a much appreciated fine tuning to this book.

Many thanks to Susan and Don Silver and Mike Moldeven who shared so much of their writing and self-publishing experiences. Their advice and direction provided invaluable assistance and time-saving tips, a necessity in my lifestyle and the essence of this book.

To my friends and fellow twenty and twenty-five year reunion committee members Isabella Barbati, Mark Friedman, Simon Grock, Dani (Vullo) Nelson, Steven Singer and John Vossler who spent many hours working on our high school reunions, thank you for your help and ideas.

Special thanks to family and friends who contributed their experiences, suggestions, efforts and editorial remarks. Grateful acknowledgements are extended to Ron and Connie Barnett, Karen Block, Harriett Goldman, Catherine Gough, Barbara Hoffman, Vivian Kahn, Judith Klonsky, Patty Krause, Lisa Raufman, Dennis Wambem, Frank Wein and Susie Zack.

And, of course, Neal and I would both like to credit our spouses, Stan Hoffman and Wendy Barnett for their important contributions and patience in seeing this project through to its completion. And finally, to my daughter Lauren, who arrived into this world in the midst of this project, you are my source of inspiration.

Linda Johnson Hoffman

Introduction

Reunions cause us to embrace many emotions, and to relive some very satisfying experiences. Most people look forward to their reunions because it provides them the opportunity to see old friends and former acquaintances, remember times past, renew relationships and form new ones. If you are planning your reunion, this book can help you to present these same opportunities in an enjoyable, entertaining and memorable atmosphere.

WHAT THIS BOOK OFFERS YOU

Putting on a reunion takes time, energy and cash-flow. But ask yourselves this, "Wouldn't you like to produce a fun-filled, personalized reunion in a minimum of time, with the least amount of effort and the lowest cost?" This guide will help you accomplish these goals.

As the title suggests, this book is designed to help make your reunion a social and financial success. A social success can be claimed when the reunion is well planned, when there is a big turnout of alumni and when guests wish it would never end. Filled with many ideas, this book will help to make your reunion a well-organized event. By implementing your own ideas along with suggestions from this book, you will find that reunion attendees will have a memorable and happy reunion experience.

A financially successful reunion will result when all costs are covered and seed money is left over for the next reunion. The recommendations in this book, including the preparation of a budget, Chapter 2, will help you achieve not only a positive ending balance, but a truly successful venture.

Definition of a Reunion

A reunion is a gathering of alumni, family, friends or associates at one time or at regular intervals. It can be any size and encompass a variety of features and activities. The focus of this book is on high school reunions but can pertain to any type of reunion, including college, family, church or other group. The high school reunion is the most common and the basis of my own experience and, therefore, is emphasized in this book. However, the majority of suggestions and recommendations described in these pages can be applied to any type of reunion by substituting the word "school" for the group you are planning to reunite.

Should I or Shouldn't I?

This book can help you make the decision to plan your reunion if you are ambivalent about taking on the challenge. Here are some solutions to two possible misgivings:

1. Why should I take on such a responsibility?

• Because everyone looks forward to their reunion, and will be grateful for all your efforts on their behalf

- Because you will gain tremendous self esteem and satisfaction knowing that you produced such a successful event
- Because in reconnecting with former classmates and reflecting on times past, you will become reacquainted with old friends and probably develop new friendships

2. *How can I find time in my busy schedule with my family, job, etc. to plan this event?*

- By organizing an effective reunion committee that works together
- By planning and prioritizing well
- By taking advantage of this reunion "how to" book for shortcuts, ideas and guidelines

If you are undecided about planning your reunion, prepare a list of PROS and CONS, as shown below:

PROS	CONS
Seeing former friends, forming new friendships	No time
Reminiscing and working together to produce a fun reunion	Not enough energy
Feeling proud of having completed a major accomplishment	Too much going on in your life right now
Having a reunion to your own liking	Never did anything like this before
Participating in a memorable experience	You don't think you will have enough assistance

PROFESSIONAL REUNION PLANNERS

When I was beginning the preparation of my twenty-year reunion, I became aware of professional reunion planners. Since there are many professional organizations that successfully plan reunions, I wanted to evaluate what they had to offer. I thought by utilizing the services of one of them, our committee could locate a high percentage of our former classmates. To get a better understanding of how the professionals performed, I called two reunion committee members from the graduating class preceding ours who had hired professional planners. Their consensus was that the planners rendered their services adequately, but former classmates had greater success locating alumni themselves, and that in the end, they spent many hours searching for them anyway.

I also learned that the professional planners were reluctant to include any additional items in their "package." For example, they would not pay the cost of creating a memory album containing alumni yearbook pictures and personal histories.

Next, I called a friend whose reunion committee had hired the same professional planners that had contacted me, and discovered the company went out of business soon after the reunion took place. Fortunately, the reunion occurred without a hitch, but the company vanished before completing the photo book. Since everything disappeared, including the negatives and proofs of the reunion photos, the alumni reunion committee had no photo album and couldn't even attempt to finish it on their own. Even worse, thousands of dollars in reunion ticket sales were lost to approximately 100 reunion committees who had hired this particular organization because the reunions had not taken place yet.

There were two additional considerations for hiring professional planners:

1. The convenience of having their staff organize and work the reception desk
2. The financial benefit of having them advance the hotel deposit for the banquet room

I reasoned that for our reunion, I could find family, friends or coworkers who would be willing to help out at the reception desk, and that by collecting advance ticket money from members of our committee, the cost of entertainment and restaurant deposits would be covered. These ideas were implemented, and with some extra effort, members of our high school class planned our own reunion.

With the assistance of this book and the computerized software program (which was created as an optional companion to this book and is described on pages 9-10), you can custom tailor your reunion to your own specifications with positive results and have a lot of fun doing it. Even if you decide to hire professional reunion planners, you can use this book in working with them.

If You Hire Professional Planners

If you find you are just not able to devote the time to planning your reunion, consider hiring professional planners. You will likely be forming a committee to hire, authorize and oversee their work, so be prepared to be involved to the extent you want a quality reunion.

You may find some professional planners willing to help with portions of your reunion such as providing the entertainment or searching for former classmates. However, **before you hire anyone, be sure to get references** from other reunion committees who have used them. Look at samples of everything they generate such as invitations, name tags and memory albums, and observe a reunion event that they organized. Also, make sure your contract with them includes your conditions. Use the following list as a guide:

The Contract with the Professional Planner

1. Secure a bond payable to the class committee should the company fail to perform. You stand to lose a lot of money, and your reunion, if the company dissolves.
2. Get copies of any alumni address lists the professional planner has as well as all alumni responses to the "missing persons list" and questionnaires. (Updates may not be easy to obtain, since this may be the basis for securing your future business.)
3. Contribute and have final approval on the design and contents of announcements, memory album and other products. Make them personal by including your own names, questionnaires and unique anecdotes.
4. Make your own choice on where to have the reunion. Many of these companies have deals worked out with certain hotels, and your preferred location may not be on their list. Remember, you get the complementary overnight room offered by most hotels to groups holding large events at the hotel.
5. Be sure the name tags include yearbook pictures.
6. See that your committee is the first to receive the unproofed reunion photo album. This is added insurance that your committee will receive the proofs should the organizers not follow through for any reason.
7. Insist that picnic details are mentioned in all mailers. (The planners may be reluctant to mention the picnic because attendance does not generate income.)
8. Be closely involved in all decision-making, including the selection of table centerpieces.

While "the professionals" may sell themselves as the answer to all your worries, remember that they have to juggle many reunions to make it economically worth their while; and, your primary interests may not be theirs.

MAKING THE DECISION TO PLAN YOUR REUNION

Taking the Plunge

Should the advantages persuade you to plan your reunion, get started on this venture right away. Once the first committee meeting takes place and everyone expresses their excitement and anticipation, you will know you made the right decision. Three tips on making the entire process run smoother include:

1. **Have Assistance.** The number of volunteers helping out can definitely aid in the success of your event. For instance, the more people searching for former classmates, the higher your turnout. Also, it is extremely helpful to have a continual flow of ideas and assistance with all assignments.

2. **Plan and Prioritize.** Plan ahead and set your priorities and goals. These attributes are essential to any successful endeavor. The outcome of your reunion will reflect your

ability to make decisions, organize well, budget appropriately
and follow through on tasks.

3. **Utilize the Optional Companion Computer Software
Program.** The computer software program is a labor saving
device and is recommended to be used with this book. It
will allow you to reach many classmates more effectively and
save you an abundance of time.

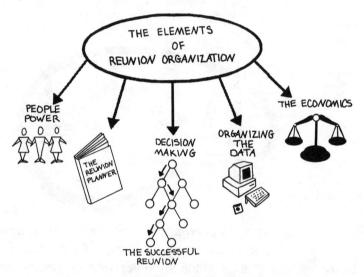

A good foundation makes planning easier and promotes success.

GETTING THE MOST VALUE FROM THIS BOOK

To get the most benefit from this book, it is recommended
that you scan through each chapter before arriving at each
time classification. This overview will prevent any surprises,
stimulate your own ideas and help you to plan ahead. The
table of contents is a complete summary of each chapter's
subject matter and, along with the index, are useful reference
guides. Especially relevant are Chapters 9 and 10, "One
Week Before the Reunion" and "The Reunion Event." Read
them well in advance of your reunion date to avoid any last

minute worries and to prepare for the time required to complete the registration process. To make your event even more special, remember to draw upon the imagination and creativity of everyone involved.

The Computer Program

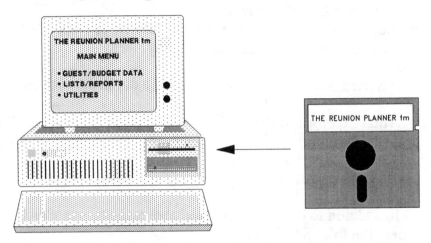

We highly recommended using the computer software program which was designed to accompany this book. Just having the program can be an incentive for planning your reunion. For easy reference, explanations on specific applications are provided throughout this book. They are encapsulated inside double-edged boxes and highlighted by a replica of a computer disk.

The Reunion Planner computer software program can simplify and streamline your reunion plan. For example, a variety of alumni lists can be created which will be extremely helpful for mailings, the phone drive and record keeping. Some lists that can be produced include the following:

• All alumni in your class
• All found alumni
• Classmates not yet found

- Interested respondents who have not paid
- All alumni who have paid

To keep track of all reunion statistics, you can quickly attain any one of the following facts:

- Total number of alumni
- Number and percentage of alumni located or responded
- Total alumni and/or guests attending

Assorted budgetary calculations can be obtained, such as:

- Total expenses to date
- Total receipts
- Current budget status
- Budget forecasts under various revenue/expense scenarios

In addition to the lists mentioned above, the program also offers the following features:

- View and print your entire alumni list or portions thereof
- Organize and use task checklists in consecutive order
- Print alumni lists in a variety of formats
- Design and print your own invitations and questionnaires
- Print names and addresses on envelopes or labels
- Print phone lists
- Print name tags
- Keep your entire alumni file on one computer disk
- Maintain accurate accounting records
- Create and tabulate a database of responses from your questionnaire

If You Do Not Have A Computer

While a computer definitely makes the job easier, this book is designed to assist reunion committees even when one is not available. You can still plan your reunion just with the aid of this book. For example, keep track of alumni information on individual index cards or other typewritten ledger. (Appendix C has sample accounting ledgers for keeping track of statistics, receipts and expenditures.) Further suggestions are offered in Chapter 2 which contains budget worksheets; and sample invitations, notices and other useful tips appear throughout this book.

HOW THIS BOOK IS STRUCTURED

This book is organized into four sections which contain chapters describing tasks that should be performed within designated time frames beginning one year before your reunion. We want to stress that **even if you do not have a year to plan your reunion, do not despair.** While this guidebook offers a variety of ideas to include in your reunion plan, you don't have to use all of them. Furthermore, you can condense the time span between the recommended periods or encourage more people to help with organizing.

The first section, GETTING ORGANIZED, begins with Chapter 1, "Twelve Months Before the Reunion." The information in this chapter presents the foundation for your reunion plan. A detailed checklist of tasks for the year then follows. Chapter 2 describes how to establish a budget.

The second section, THE FOOTWORK, includes Chapter 3 which offers ideas for achieving a good turnout. Chapters 4 through 6 present assignments to perform in nine, six and three months before the reunion.

The third section, THE COUNTDOWN, identifies tasks to be handled in the final month prior to the reunion, and are explained in Chapters 7 through 9. A complete profile of the registration process is included in Chapter 9.

The final section entitled REUNION DAY AND AFTERWARDS, provides a suggested preview of reunion day activities in Chapter 10, and offers comments on closing procedures and ideas for your next reunion in Chapter 11.

As part of the development of this book, a questionnaire was distributed to various people requesting information and opinions on their reunion experiences. Responses to the survey provided more useful ideas including where to hold reunions, examples of reunion activities, ice breakers and many other tips which are included in this book.

A reunion survey is at the end of this book. We would like to hear from you and about your reunion and would like to include some of your reunion experiences in the next edition of this book. Please take a moment to complete the survey and return it to us in care of the publisher:

GOODMAN LAUREN PUBLISHING
11661 San Vicente Blvd. Suite 505
Los Angeles, California 90049

OVERVIEW

The successful planning of your reunion will be based upon the amount of time you and other volunteers commit to it. Having the time to devote to this project may seem difficult, but all you need to do is set aside some evenings and weekends. Author Susan Silver, *Organized to be the Best!*, explains that, "Time management is the foundation of good organization." You need to "take the time to plan and prioritize" to be successful with your goals because "research indicates that for every hour of planning, you save three or four hours." By following this guide and planning carefully, your reunion will be a well-organized, memorable event.

GETTING ORGANIZED

1   **Twelve Months Before the Reunion**   15
        Reunion Checklist   31
2   **The Budget**   35

Chapter 1

Twelve Months Before The Reunion

THE GROUNDWORK IN THREE STEPS

While it may seem far away, don't wait much longer than a year before your reunion to get started on the three basic steps outlined in this chapter. *Making key contacts, beginning the search for alumni and deciding when and where to have the reunion* are three primary activities in planning a reunion. All other aspects of planning will be better accomplished with the assistance of a reunion committee, however, these first few exercises can be handled by one or two people.

STEP 1. Make Key Contacts

Two key contacts should be made early on in the preparation stage. One is with your high school and the other is with various former members of your class to establish a reunion committee.

The School

Your school is a valuable resource for planning your reunion. It would be wise to pay a personal visit there for

several reasons. You may find more useful information and
lists, acquire interesting written material or even have an
encounter with a former teacher (all of which won't occur
over the phone). Some acquisitions may include the
following:

1. Any alumni data:
*   A graduation list with the names and addresses at the
    time of graduation (depending on the number of years
    out of high school, you will find many parents still reside
    at the same address)
*   Diploma list or cards
*   Enrollment cards
*   Any information with dates of birth, (this will be helpful
    when researching voter registration lists and marriage
    license bureaus)
*   Any data with the first names of both parents. This will
    help locate alumni when searching telephone directories

Enter any known parent's names as the
alternate contact. This address will
print on the labels until a current one
is known. Then the program will default
to the new address in future mailings.

---

2. A meeting with the reunion coordinator to familiarize
    yourself with the school's staff and procedures on
    handling reunion information
3. A tour of the high school grounds
4. Written messages from alumni who may have called in
    seeking reunion information
5. Copies of the school song, yearbook and other
    memorabilia
6. Ideas for decorations, banners and other displays

7. School identified items from the student store such as hats, pencils, t-shirts or other memorabilia that could be displayed at the reunion or raffled to raise additional funds

One reunion committee chair got a lot more than she expected from a visit to her former alma mater:

> I got more information (I already had the graduation list from our previous reunion) and assistance from a visit to my high school when I began planning my twenty-five year reunion. I met the reunion coordinator who was very helpful. She gave me messages on reunion inquiries from alumni of my class, a copy of our school song and even suggestions for places to hold reunions near the area. I learned that if we wanted to have a picnic on the high school grounds, a date needed to be reserved very soon, even though our reunion was a year away.
>
> I also heard that the student store carried stuffed animal replicas of our high school mascot. I contemplated using them as table centerpieces, auctioning them off at the reunion and buying a nice gift for the high school with the proceeds. The student store had even more wonders to behold. They had one yearbook left from our class graduation year. Knowing this book would be in high demand by alumni who had since lost theirs, I purchased it. I also found items I could use for decorations including a t-shirt, pencils and notebooks.
>
> With a visitor's pass, I then wandered through the school's halls and buildings for a nostalgic encounter with the past. Upon learning of the presence of a former gym teacher still at the school, I walked to her office and shared an informal chat about the school, the students and the changing times. All in all, it was a very rewarding visit.

Continue the Contact Throughout the Year. The high school is an important link for alumni to learn of any impending reunion plans. To facilitate this process, and prevent any potential misinformation, follow through with updates on the reunion throughout the coming year. Here are some ideas:

- Design and send several flyers or other conspicuous reminders.

ANNOUNCING...

FAIRVIEW HIGH SCHOOL
CLASS OF 1972
20 YEAR REUNION

Please direct any inquiries
To the Reunion Committee
Jane Davidson (213)555-5555
Jeff Scott (818)666-6666

Thank You   *October 2, 1991*

Figure 1-1. Sample flyer to send to the high school administrative office

- Call the high school periodically to check that correct information is being distributed about your reunion. The high school administrative staff may change, and reunion information may get muddled in the process, especially if the reunion coordinator is not available or there is no specific person to direct inquiries.
- Closer to the reunion date, send copies of newspaper ads about your reunion.
- See if the school will post a notice on the outside marquis or billboard at the high school.

Establish the Reunion Committee

While there are usually one or two persons from any class who might initiate a reunion drive, it is highly recommended that a reunion committee be formed in order to provide more assistance on all other aspects of planning the reunion such as those listed below:

Additional Responsibilities That Need to be Handled

1. Finding alumni
2. Sending out reunion announcements
3. Editing the alumni histories for the Memory Album
4. Preparing the Memory Album
5. Finding entertainment
6. Planning additional entertainment features such as a picnic, pre-event fund raiser or three-day event
7. Sending out payment acknowledgment postcards and reminder notices
8. Publicizing reunion announcements, including media ads
9. Typing alumni information on the photo cards
10. Preparing a slide show or video tape for viewing at the reunion
11. Helping with the phone bank
12. Arranging for door prize donations
13. Designing custom tickets
14. Ordering the banner
15. Creating a business directory with alumni business cards
16. Organizing statistics for any database or survey that you might conduct
17. Collecting nostalgia items for the "memory table"
18. Creating table centerpieces, banner, room decorations
19. Design a program
20. Event set up
21. Registration procedures
    a. make name tags
    b. assemble the registration envelopes
22. Preparing the photo book
23. Establishing and processing a donation or gift to the high school

"Going it alone," that is, if only one person intends to plan the reunion, will be difficult (especially if it is a large reunion). You need a committee just to maintain the enthusiasm and energy level essential in organizing any event. In setting up a committee, try to pick those people who have time, talent and a genuine interest in making your reunion work. Your best source of assistance is former classmates. Four recommendations are offered:

1. Enlist the assistance of high school classmates you still keep in touch with and you know will be enthusiastic.
2. You may find that someone contacted the school expressing interest in helping with reunion planning.
3. Former class officers or reunion committee members might be eager to help.
4. Request assistance in your mailings.

STEP 2. Search For Alumni

The First Committee Meeting. Initially, many concerns will arise besides planning the reunion.

It will be natural to reminisce during the first committee meeting, however, try to exercise some restraint to get the important tasks done. You can accomplish a lot in just two or three meetings geared to the alumni search and mailings. Meetings usually occur at the chairperson's home. If that is not a convenient place for follow up meetings, or you need more space for the mailing meetings, meet in the evening at a committee member's office, or perhaps your selected hotel has a conference room you can use.

Your main focus for the first committee meeting should be on accomplishing two goals:

* organizing the search for alumni
* collecting seed money for initial expenses

In order to maximize your time with productive results, try to have enough assistance. One or two people will likely emerge as the leaders and take responsibility for delegating tasks. If you are the main organizer, you must follow up to make sure people are getting things done, especially the most time-consuming task, locating alumni. Reaching a majority of alumni is essential to have a good turnout. This will be accomplished by the amount of effort placed in searching for alumni.

In preparing the alumni lists to give to committee members, make sure to request that returned reports with updated data is clear and legible. Divide the list of names among the volunteers. Remind callers to request information on other alumni as calls are made. Reimburse volunteers for phone calls when you get enough seed money.

The computerized alumni list will have all known names, addresses and phone numbers. The list can be printed by area code for the convenience and cost savings in phone calls to the committee members.

THE REUNION PLANNER tm

Some people will never bother to find out about their reunions unless someone has contacted **them.** As hard as it is to find people, and as much as someone would like to attend, many alumni will fail to make an effort to call the high school to find out about a reunion, but will be extremely happy to be "found." Hence, a large part of planning a reunion is in searching for alumni.

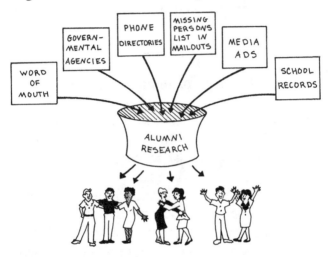

Begin the Search. **Thorough investigative work will result in many happy reunions.**

According to research, the greatest percentage of people still live within 50 miles of the school they attended. If you know the graduate's first, middle and last names as well as their parent's first names, you will have a distinct advantage in locating people. First, have volunteers contact anyone else they know, then try some of the following methods:

- Search through local and outlying area telephone books. You can find phone books and a zip code directory for all of the United States in your larger public libraries.

- Contact the parents of alumni.

- The County Assessor's office has property tax records. For no cost, you can research through an alphabetical listing of properties which includes names and addresses.

- The County Registrar of Voters is also accessible and free. Registered voters are listed with names, addresses and birthdates. Phone numbers are sometimes included.

- The Department of Motor Vehicles has a search service for a minimum fee per name. They provide addresses for requests with full names and birthdates. This access is not available in some states.

- County Marriage License Bureaus are good for finding the married names of the female members of your class.

- The County Hall of Records has public birth records. Parents' full names and addresses are recorded with the child's name.

- Referral requests during phone drives and a "Missing Alumni" list in your mailers are excellent resources.

- University alumni records for colleges nearby your high school may yield more information if you know the colleges your classmates intended to attend.

- Class reunion committees of earlier years may have brothers or sisters of members of your class and could provide further information.

Input any current information into your database right away. The number of returned letters will be reduced by having your address list as current as possible for the first mailing.

THE REUNION PLANNER tm

While trying to locate and notify alumni about the reunion, callers may encounter some apathetic responses. Dealing with reluctant reunion attendees is a complex subject and compelling enough to be thoroughly reviewed. Chapter 3 covers this topic. Have each committee member searching for alumni read Chapter 3 for ideas in responding to apprehensive alumni.

Seed Money

Since there will be postage, phone and stationery costs as well as deposits to the hotel and entertainment, the committee will need some initial financing. Ask committee members to pay for their tickets now or grant a loan to the committee, or, plan a fund raiser. To obtain initial funding for one 25 year reunion, here is what one committee did:

> We held a small spaghetti dinner fund raiser at an Italian restaurant and charged $25.00 per person. Announcements for this event, which was limited to 100 persons, were included with the first reunion mailing. The event was a huge success, it was sold out with many alumni being be turned away.

STEP 3. Decide When and Where to Have the Reunion

Try to make these two decisions a year in advance of your reunion before locations are reserved by other groups. For additional input, or to get indications of your classmates' preferences, send out an early questionnaire to alumni 18 to 24 months before the reunion (see Appendix A, page 131 for a sample mailer).

Set the Date

This decision may be determined by your chosen location's availability. Reunions are generally planned during the summer months, June through September, however, reunions occur throughout the year. Pick a date you feel would most benefit your group. For example, select a date that would enable families to plan vacations around school breaks. Year end holidays and three day weekends are not good since they are usually busy with family events.

Depending on the time of year, you could plan your reunion around a theme. Decorations, name tags and invitations can display the appropriate accents. A "dress-as-you-did-in-high-school" reunion is one idea. If your reunion is in July, consider a Fourth of July reunion decor. If your reunion is in October, a Halloween theme could be explored; an early February date could favor a Valentine's Day theme. Or, make up your own theme that has relevance to your class such as a "1950's Sock Hop" reunion. These are just a few suggestions. A theme party is not typical, but it offers some variation on the routine.

Choose the place

Hotels with large banquet facilities are the most popular places to hold reunions. Depending upon the place you choose, food will either be provided in-house, or catered. Remember, the most important aspect of a reunion is to offer a comfortable environment and pleasant atmosphere for alumni to be able to talk. Everything else is secondary. An expensive dinner/dance event needn't be planned for every reunion. Whatever you organize, base your decision on how much your budget allows. It might be worthwhile to prepare a preliminary budget (see Chapter 2 "The Budget") before making a decision.

Take a list of questions you want answered while interviewing prospective places to hold your reunion (see list on next page). Be sure to look at each location you are considering before making a decision. Your selected place may be based upon such site factors as the look of the banquet room, the size of the reception area or just the overall "feel" of the surroundings. Be prepared with a figure for an estimated turnout. (See Chapter 2, page 36, for assistance on estimating a turnout.)

Proposed List of Questions To Ask the Catering Manager:

1. Look at the available rooms; see if there is a separate area where alumni can sit and talk away from the music.

2. Is the reception area separate from the dining room? Can reception tables and chairs be provided, and where would they be located?

3. Is there a spacious/separate area for the photographer?

4. Obtain the list of menus and prices. What will be the final total price per person including tax and tip?

5. What are the different meal options? For example, sit down, buffet or a choice of several food stations?

6. Can we bring our own table wine?

7. Is there a cash minimum for total bar sales, and how much is charged if the minimum is not met? Will the committee be reimbursed a percentage of the bar sales sold above a base amount?

8. Do you have suggestions for bands, disc jockeys, photographers or florists?

9. How many extra meals can be provided above the original guarantee?

10. Can you provide bulletin boards and easels?

11. Can your staff hang a banner for us? Where? Can we put up posters and other decorations?

12. Can a podium with a microphone be provided?

13. Is a television set and VCR available to show a video? If not, can one be easily set up?

14. (If a slide show is planned) Can a projector and screen be provided? Check that the room has enough electrical outlets and wattage to accommodate all your needs.

15. How soon can we decorate? How late can we have the room?

16. (Hotels only) Is a room offered with the event? What room discounts are available for guests attending the reunion? Do you have a flyer we could include in our mailings?

17. (If the required deposit is too high) Can the deposit be paid in two or three installments?

18. When is the final meal count and payment expected?

19. Is there handicapped accessibility? Non-smoking area? Hat and coat check in?

20. What is the parking situation? How much is valet parking? Is there self-parking?

21. _____

_____

If there is a room you like, reserve it as soon as possible. If you want your reunion in May or June, remember that these months are popular for weddings, proms and graduation parties, so reserve early. On the other hand, don't make a hasty decision. Visit different locations if you are not completely satisfied. Catering managers want your business as much as you want a location for your reunion, so don't be forced into making a quick decision if the manager wants immediate confirmation. Tentatively reserve the room while you look at other sites.

Places to Hold Your Reunion

Restaurants/Hotels/Country Clubs. These are obvious first choices since they have convenient ballrooms and banquet facilities. Establishments such as these usually have a wide selection of menus and prices. In choosing a menu, be sure to add sales tax and gratuity when determining the total cost per person. A sample menu might look like this:

Dinner cost:	$22.00
Sales Tax @ 8%:	1.76
Gratuity @ 17%:	4.03
Total Cost Per Person:	$27.79

One advantage in having your reunion at a hotel is that a free overnight room is usually provided for major events. The complementary room could be the committee's room to use to coordinate and change clothes. Also, ask about a reimbursement if bar sales go above a base amount.

Yacht Cruise. If you live near a marina, you can charter a yacht and cruise the waters for several hours. This may be expensive since the cost of food is added to the yacht rental fee. However, you could lower the total cost by just serving finger food and dessert. As of April, 1992, one yacht charter organization in Marina del Rey, California charged the following fees for a chartered cruise for four hours serving a Mexican meal buffet for 150 guests:

Yacht Rental:	$3,550
Mexican meal including loading fee, servers, tax and tip @ $21 per person:	$3,150
Total Cost:	$6,700

Per Person Cost (Cruise and Food): $45

If this idea appeals to you, contact the local Marina's information center or look in the Yellow Pages under Boat Charters and compare prices.

Mansions/Estates/Museums/Art Galleries. Your local Chamber of Commerce may have a list of mansions, estates or designer showcase homes that can be rented for such occasions. Many museums and art galleries also rent their premises for parties. Food, refreshments, servers, tables and chairs, insurance and clean up costs are usually extra. The expense can be minimized, however, by just having finger food and dessert, and by supplying your own bar. Just obtain a liquor license for a day. Check with your state's Alcoholic Beverage Control Department for procedures. Purchase your own liquor and hire a professional bartender. A friend or family member can help out by selling drink tickets. Call a few restaurants and hotels for ideas on amounts of liquor to purchase for your estimated attendance.

Theme Park or Dinner House Theater. Many theme parks (e.g. Disneyland, Universal Studios) and dinner house theaters have "party packages" with accessibility to entertainers, video specialists, etc. You can probably negotiate a group discount rate at a nearby hotel for guests who require overnight accomodations. You may even be able to arrange free shuttle service to and from the reunion if you can guarantee a large block of rooms.

Picnic or Beach Party. This is a great choice for a more casual reunion where alumni can bring their families. All you need is a spacious area with picnic tables and barbecue facilities. Picnic areas and baseball diamonds in city operated parks should be reserved quite early.

High school gym, field or hall. Consider having a reunion at your former high school. See if your school would be willing to let you use the grounds, hall or gymnasium for your reunion. Rent a jukebox and serve finger sandwiches and dessert. Guests could come dressed in high school garb and play basketball. This could be an inexpensive interim 5 year reunion between two dinner/dance reunions. You may not be able to serve alcohol on these premises, however.

Camps/Conference Centers/Lodges. Plan a day long outing or a weekend retreat. A university or private conference center, camp, or youth hostel may have facilities for such events. Try calling club associations, organizational lodges or universities to see if they have such accommodations.

Weekend Combination of Events. Continue your reunion throughout the weekend with several different events.

> A high school in Atlantic City, New Jersey, celebrated their twenty-fifth reunion starting with a Friday night get-together over wine and cheese at the high school and included a tour of the school. On Saturday, former members of the school's basketball team organized a game at the school. That evening, a dinner/dance was held at a local hotel. A picnic at a local beach occurred on Sunday.

Offering a little variety in your reunion activities allows people with scheduling conflicts or financial concerns to attend at least one of the gatherings. In addition, a casual pre-reunion get together could be just the trick to ease reunion anxieties.

"It was a terrific ice-breaker," according to a reunion goer from Van Nuys High School in California. "We had a casual pre-reunion cocktail party on Friday night in the Hospitality Suite provided by the hotel sponsoring the dinner/dance on Saturday night. Alumni who weren't hotel guests came too." Other possible locations for a pre-reunion event might be the gym at your school or in the hotel lounge where the main event is being held. All sorts of possibilities are imaginable for a weekend of reminiscing and activities.

REUNION CHECKLIST

Twelve Months Before the Reunion --- Chapter 1

_____Make key contacts
　　_____call the high school
　　_____set up alumni committee
_____Arrange the first committee meeting
　　_____coordinate the search for former classmates
　　_____collect seed money
_____Decide when and where to have the reunion

The Budget --- Chapter 2

_____Set up a budget
　　_____estimate turnout
　　_____estimate expenses
　　_____estimate ticket price

Nine Months Before the Reunion --- Chapter 4

_____Prepare the first announcement
_____Order rubber stamp with the committee's
return address, or buy labels, or have the address
printed on envelopes
_____Plan a committee mailing meeting and send out
the first announcement

_____Select the entertainment
_____Check costs for professional video and/or slide show
_____Choose the photographer
_____Plan the picnic
_____Open up a bank account
_____Make files for organizing the paperwork

Six Months Before the Reunion --- Chapter 5

_____Update alumni list
_____Begin preparation of the memory album
_____Plan the name tags
_____Design second mailing
_____prepare list of unfound alumni
_____Plan mailing meeting and send out second
    announcement
_____Print payment acknowledgement postcards
_____Plan and design tickets
_____Set up accounting ledger

Three Months Before the Reunion --- Chapter 6

_____Update alumni list
_____Edit the alumni histories for the memory album
_____Begin phone drive
_____Send announcements to local newspapers and
    radio stations
_____Plan table centerpieces and other reunion decor
_____Order banner
_____Order movie posters or picture blowups
_____Plan nostalgia table
_____Find T-shirt vendor and provide list of alumni names
_____Arrange for reception desk workers

One Month Before the Reunion --- Chapter 7

_____Continue phone drive, update alumni list
_____Edit alumni histories for memory album
_____Send reminder notices
_____Make name tags
_____Create a printed program
_____Prepare spoken program notes
_____Prepare announcements
_____select winners of awards
_____Buy door prizes and awards
_____Prepare photo collage, signs and door prize coupons
_____Type up photo cards

Two Weeks Before the Reunion --- Chapter 8

_____Verify attendance data, print list of paid guests
_____Verify attendance of reception desk workers
_____Check on floral arrangements or prepare your table centerpieces
_____Confirm attendance of entertainer, videographer, photographer, T-shirt vendor
_____Verify attendance and, if appropriate, make hotel arrangements for special guests
_____Finalize program announcements and award winners
_____Verify delivery of donated door prizes
_____Proof memory album draft and other handout and give camera-ready artwork to printer
_____Mail tickets

One Week Before the Reunion --- Chapter 9

_____Prepare final list of paid attendees
_____Prepare registration packets
_____will call
_____pre-paid ticket holders

_____ Make any other necessary signs, e.g. letters for
the registration tables

_____ Give meal count and balance of money to restaurant

_____ Verify with the banquet manager that all requested
items will be there including: registration tables,
easels, bulletin boards, microphone and podium

_____ Have a contingency plan for someone else to take
over your responsibilities, just in case you are
(heaven forbid) unable to attend

The Reunion Event --- Chapter 10

_____ Bring **Reunion Day Necessities** list

_____ Retrieve supplies at end of reunion

_____ For the picnic: bring banner, lunch, sports
equipment

After the Reunion --- Chapter 11

_____ Prepare photo album and send to photographer

_____ Send thank you notes

_____ Send out memory albums and photo books to those
who didn't attend

_____ Close bank account after all checks have cleared

_____ Store reunion supplies in easy and safe place

_____ Complete and send in Reunion Survey on page 125

Chapter 2

The Budget

Two important reasons for creating a budget are the following:

1. To determine an appropriate ticket price.
2. To make financial projections to insure that expenses are covered and there is a positive ending balance.

Use the sample budget worksheet on page 37 as a guide, and create a preliminary budget using your own figures on the worksheet on page 38. Make several copies of this page, or use a pencil, as you will likely be making changes. *The Reunion Planner Computer Program* has a budget model for estimating and keeping track of receipts and expenditures, as well as being able to make various budgetary projections (see page 44). However, planners without a computer can use the accounting ledger which appears in Appendix C as a guide.

Your budget should contain the following categories and estimations:

ASSUMPTIONS

Total Class Membership. Enter the number of students in your class. Your high school will have this answer for you.

Estimated Turnout.   In determining your expected attendance, be conservative in your approach because a slight underestimation of guests is more manageable in choosing what size banquet room you will need.   A restaurant or hotel can always add a few more tables, but a large room with few tables is not very cozy. Various factors can be used to estimate your attendance including: **the size of your graduating class; attendance at the last reunion; time between reunions (a shorter time frame between reunions will likely bring fewer alumni); and, the number of people helping to locate alumni.**   For more help on determining a turnout, you could contact reunion committees from previous graduating classes, or ask the catering managers of several large local hotels/restaurants that handle reunions.

A method we used for our twentieth reunion turned out to be very accurate. We took 40 percent of our class size, or 200, including spouses.   We figured more people would attend our twenty-year reunion since it had been ten years since the previous one when 150 guests arrived. There were 208 in attendance for our twenty-year reunion. You may have another method for calculating an expected turnout. However, for our sample budget, 40% is used.

Estimated Alumni. You will also need to estimate an alumni turnout to determine the number of individual items to prepare, such as memory albums, programs and photo books and if applicable, a parking cost. In the sample budget, 65% of the estimated turnout, or 130 alumni, was used.

SAMPLE BUDGET

ASSUMPTIONS

Total Class Membership	500
Estimated Turnout (Alumni & Guests -- @ 40%)	200
Estimated Alumni Turnout (@ 65%)	130
Tables Required (@ 10 people per table)	20

ESTIMATED EXPENSES

ITEM	UNIT COST	PER ITEM	TOTAL NUMBER	ESTIMATED COST
Dinner (Incl. Tax & Tip)	$ 34.00	person	200	$ 6800.
Entertainment	600.00	group	1	600
Postage	.29	envelope	1200	348
Stationery	200.00	event	1	200
Name Tags	1.00	person	200	200
Printing	200.00	event	1	200
Memory Albums	5.00	alumnus	130	650
Photo Books	4.00	alumnus	130	520
Table Centerpieces	10.00	table	20	200
Decorations	50.00	event	1	50
Door Prizes	15.00	prize	6	90
Slide Show	2000.00	event	1	2000
Programs	2.00	alumnus	130	260
Workers at Reception Desk	18.00	worker	3	54
Parking	2.50	car	130	325
Business Directory	1.00		130	130
Misc	300.00		1	300

Total Expenses: $ 12,927

ESTIMATED REVENUES

ITEM	UNIT AMOUNT	PER ITEM	TOTAL NUMBER	ESTIMATED COST
Ticket Sales	55	person	200	$ 11,000
Memory Albums	10	alumnus	20	200
Photo Books	5	alumnus	20	100
Business Directory	10	card	50	500

Total Revenues: $ 11,800

Balance: $ (1,127)

Balance without slideshow $ 873

BUDGET WORKSHEET

ASSUMPTIONS

Total Class Membership   _____
Estimated Turnout (Alumni & Guests -- @ ___%)   _____
Estimated Alumni Turnout (@ ___%)   _____
Tables Required (@ ___ people per table)   _____

ESTIMATED EXPENSES

ITEM	UNIT COST	PER ITEM	TOTAL NUMBER	ESTIMATED COST
Dinner (Incl. Tax & Tip)	$ _____	person	_____	$ _____
Entertainment	_____	group	_____	_____
Postage	_____	envelope	_____	_____
Stationery	_____	event	_____	_____
Name Tags	_____	person	_____	_____
Printing	_____	event	_____	_____
Memory Albums	_____	alumnus	_____	_____
Photo Books	_____	alumnus	_____	_____
Table Centerpieces	_____	table	_____	_____
Decorations	_____	event	_____	_____
Door Prizes	_____	prize	_____	_____
Slide Show	_____	event	_____	_____
Programs	_____	alumnus	_____	_____
Workers at Reception Desk	_____	worker	_____	_____
Parking	_____	car	_____	_____
_____	_____	_____	_____	_____
_____	_____	_____	_____	_____
_____	_____	_____	_____	_____

Total Expenses: $ _____

ESTIMATED REVENUES

ITEM	UNIT AMOUNT	PER ITEM	TOTAL NUMBER	ESTIMATED COST
Ticket Sales	_____	person	_____	$ _____
Memory Albums	_____	alumnus	_____	_____
Photo Books	_____	alumnus	_____	_____
_____	_____	_____	_____	_____
_____	_____	_____	_____	_____

Total Revenues: $ _____

Balance: $ _____

Tables. Divide the expected turnout by 10, a standard number of seats per table. You now have an approximate number of tables for determining how many centerpieces will be needed.

ESTIMATED EXPENSES

Room rental cost, meal costs and entertainment. If you chose a hotel or restaurant, the dance floor, tables and chairs, utensils, table linens, waiters and bartenders (above a minimum in bar sales) are included in the total meal cost. However, if you select a facility that requires you to rent these items, add these costs to your budget.

Once the place and menu have been chosen, you will have the most necessary and largest reunion expense determined. (Be sure to include tax and tip in the total cost per person.) The entertainment cost can be determined by asking various professional disc jockeys (D.Js). (For help on finding musicians, see page 63.) In our example, $600 was used as an average cost for hiring a D.J. in the Los Angeles area.

Stationery, printing and postage. Stationery, envelopes, postcards, name tags, tickets and printing costs can be estimated according to your class size. Postage costs in our example were estimated for a class of 500 and were based on five different mailings:

1. 500 letters to the entire class
2. A 300 piece second mailing to the class. This is reduced assuming a third of the envelopes in the first mailer is returned with incorrect or unforwardable addresses
3. 130 acknowledgement postcards to ticket purchasers
4. 150 reminder postcards
5. Envelopes with tickets, 130

Under this scenario, at $.29 per each envelope and postcard, postage would be $348. Postcards cost slightly less to mail, however, for estimating purposes, use first class amounts.

Memory album, photo book, table centerpieces and other displays. In estimating a cost for these items, for now, use an amount you foresee spending. For example, a memory album prepared by the committee may only bear a printing cost. The cost of a reunion photo book can range between $5.00 and $13.00, so call various reunion photographers for quotations. If you got a brochure from professional reunion planners you interviewed, call the photographer they use.

If you want flowers as table centerpieces, local florists can quote you prices. If you design your own centerpieces, you could save money. If you want balloons, call local party stores for the cost of renting a helium tank. Once final selections are made, the true costs for these items can replace the estimated ones. The budget can then be reevaluated and, if necessary, adjusted.

Other decorations, such as items purchased at the student store, posters, balloons, frames for a photo collage, in-memorandum display and other memorabilia, can be computed by calling various vendors for prices.

Additional expenses. Extra costs such as door prizes, slide show, video tapes, parking fees and paid workers at the reception desk should be included in your preliminary budget to have the cash available if you are at all considering them. In the sample budget, three workers were budgeted at $6.00 per hour for three hours at the reception desk for a total of $54.00. To determine parking costs, the estimated alumni attendance, 130, was multiplied by a parking fee of $2.50 per car for a total estimated parking expense of $325.

Door prizes, awards or reception worker costs can be reduced or eliminated if you can get them donated or the services volunteered. A category for miscellaneous expenses, of approximately two to three percent should also be included in your budget. Such unforseen charges might include bank account fees, insurance, long distance phone calls, complementary dinners and/or hotel rooms or tips.

Total Expenses. In the sample budget, total expenses are estimated at $12,927 or about $65.00 per person. The ticket price is considered too high (we remembered that alumni will likely be spending even more money to attend the reunion), so some costs must be reduced or eliminated.

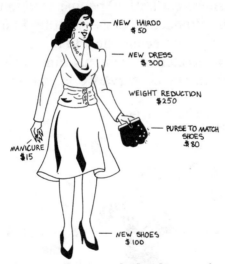

Going to a reunion contributes to the local economic prosperity.

ESTIMATED REVENUES

Choose a ticket price that will cover all your estimated expenses. **Remember that you have to consider a price that a majority of people would consider affordable.** In our example, we chose $55.00 per person anticipating that this

was the maximum we could charge and the minimum we had
to have to pay for the basic features we wanted.

Total Revenues. The figure for total revenues will be based
mainly on ticket receipts. Any proceeds from sales of
memory albums or photo books will be insignificant since
only alumni not attending the main event would purchase
them. There will be added income based on a higher ticket
price for late purchasers, however, it is recommended that
you use one base ticket price when computing revenues.

Advertising income could be generated by creating a
business directory and charging for example, $10.00 to
display each business card. If 50 people send in their cards,
you collect $500. Production costs might be $1.00 per book
or $130. It is even more economical to place these card ads
in your photo book/memory album. Since this additional
revenue is uncertain, be conservative in your estimate.

Balancing the Budget. Remember, the revenues from ticket sales must
cover all expenses.

ESTIMATED BALANCE

Subtract the estimated costs from estimated revenues. In the sample budget, every possible cost was included, and the balance resulted in a negative $1,127. This meant that some costs had to be deleted or reduced. Costs can be adjusted or eliminated, however, you must remember that once a ticket price has been selected, this will be a cap for determining revenues. When the slide show was eliminated, a surplus of $873 was realized. The surplus meant we could afford more elaborate centerpieces, a more professional looking memory album, another specialty item or have seed money for the next reunion.

Raising Additional Cash

You should always have a positive ending balance. However, if you still find yourselves short of cash, and you don't want to eliminate any costs, try organizing a fund raiser like the one described on page 24 early on in the planning stage. Please don't ask for money at the reunion to cover expenses. This looks like sloppy management and is a negative approach. Furthermore, attendees will most likely be reluctant to contribute at this point.

A raffle can be organized by substituting one of the donated door prizes or getting something donated prior to the event. A dinner for two at a nice restaurant or tickets to some theatrical event or theme park could be arranged by making a few phone calls and offering free advertisement in your memory album or other display at the reunion. Charge a modest amount, such as $1.00 per ticket. Have someone sell tickets at the reception desk next to a large sign, and announce the raffle during dinner also. You can select the winner during the program.

Last minute funds could also be raised by charging a little extra for items sold at the reunion like T-shirts, videos or other souvenirs. If the vendor is handling sales, ask a friend or family member to assist with cataloging the sales. Another suggestion: auction off the table centerpieces.

If you are working with professional planners, and need additional funds to pay for an item you would like to offer that wouldn't be included in the "package deal," work out an arrangement whereby they charge a few dollars extra for each ticket and reimburse the committee the overage.

THE COMPUTER PROGRAM'S BUDGET REPORT

If you have *The Reunion Planner* computer software, input your assumptions for all expenses and revenues. You can then come up with several budget scenarios. For example, if you estimate 150 people will be attending at a ticket cost of $50.00 per person, $7,500 will be generated in revenues. Upon entering your estimated expenses, you can adjust costs or the ticket price until a positive ending balance is achieved.

A nice feature in the computer program's budget is that it offers an accounting analysis for both an estimated and actual financial standing. To be more specific, as you enter revenues received and expenses incurred, the program transfers the information into a file that will display your current budget account status. This report can be balanced against your bank account statement. Then, as actual expense dollars become known, this information can be entered into your estimated budget to have a more accurate appraisal of your budget forecast.

THE FOOTWORK

3   How To Increase Attendance   47
4   Nine Months Before the Reunion   57
5   Six Months Before the Reunion   69
6   Three Months Before the Reunion   79

Chapter 3

How To Increase Attendance

A reunion is most exciting when a large representation of your alumni is in attendance. Moreover, reunion memories are more cherished as the ratio of recognizable guests increase. One of your goals, as most reunion organizers would agree, is to have as many alumni that can be located attend the reunion. A high turnout will result through careful investigation and perseverance. Ideas for locating alumni are covered in Chapter 1. This chapter concentrates on how to stimulate and encourage those alumni **that have already been located** to come to the reunion.

PORTRAY AN ENTICING REUNION

There are a variety of ways to make your reunion appear as the event not to be missed.

Correspondence

Communication through the mail is the most popular method used to notify alumni about a reunion. Try to make the notices informational and interesting.

1. Include alumni by soliciting their ideas on possible facilities or on the entertainment. Send out a questionnaire before you start planning the event. You may get some good ideas and alumni will feel they participated in the planning. (See a sample early mailer in Appendix A.)

2. Make the mailers eye-catching by including illustrations such as your high school emblem or mascot, or use computer graphics clip art (if you have access to a computer). If a theme party like a "sock hop" is planned, include drawings on the mailers embellishing the theme. One reunion planner who is an attorney wrote the reunion announcement as a court summons. This definitely grabbed people's attention. But remember you not only want to attract attention, you also want to provide useful information and elicit positive reactions.

Phone Calls

Follow-up phone calls to those alumni who have not responded to written correspondence provide that extra personal touch by letting people know that their presence is desired at the reunion. Phone calls are especially important if you are working with professional reunion organizers. Alumni might not respond to a written invitation, but may be encouraged to attend upon receiving a phone call from another alumni.

In addition to making personal contact, the phone drive will provide more information on the whereabouts of other members of your class. Therefore, remind people making calls to ask for information on other alumni. Continue the calls as close to the reunion as possible, because many people decide to attend only days before the reunion. More descriptions for forming a phone bank appear in Chapter 6.

Entertainment

Exciting musical entertainment may spruce up the event. If there are any special appearances, be sure to mention them in the reunion mailings. Be sure to utilize whatever contacts or ideas your reunion committee or alumni may have in selecting the entertainment.

- A musical group that was popular during your high school years may be available. If you find a group you liked, ask if they could perform for a modest fee. The worst they can do is say no.

- Approach a popular radio disk jockey that may still be in the public domain. He or she may be available to make a special appearance, to present awards or to introduce your program speakers.

- Hire a professional "look-a-like," or have someone you know dress up as a well-known person (politician, teacher or pop singer from your era) and walk around talking to people all evening.

- Hire a mime to joke around with the guests. They wouldn't be interrupting your reunion ambiance, and might liven up the festivities.

- Employ a caricaturist to walk around the room and draw pictures of the guests. You could have this in lieu of a photographer for variety.

Special Guests

The attendance of well-liked high school teachers or coaches may induce alumni to come to the reunion.

At our twenty-year reunion, we invited a well-liked football coach who retired the same year our class graduated. Well, twenty years later, looking terrific and fit as ever, Coach Nelson agreed to attend our reunion. His 84th birthday was on the same day as our reunion. During the program he came to the podium and, to everyone's delight, led us into his famous, rousing "Nelson Yell" exactly as he'd done during football games in high school. After that we sang "Happy Birthday" to him. He seemed to be quite touched and happy. Everyone admitted it was a highlight of the evening.

DEALING WITH RELUCTANT REUNION ATTENDEES

Undoubtedly, as you contact alumni you will find that some people are reluctant to attend their reunion aside from the usual unavailability due to geographical, financial or timing constraints. While incomprehensible to you, disinterest is one problem all reunion organizers face.

It can be disappointing to encounter indifference from former classmates. Our reunion committee wanted all the alumni we could find to attend. After all, we were working very hard to make this an enjoyable and memorable event. However, throughout our phone drive we discovered that some alumni were reluctant to attend. Apprehensions ranged from disinterest to reluctance at being seen. Such anxieties could stem from high school insecurities, current fears that they might not be as successful or look as good as they would like. We tried to explain that everyone has changed since high school and that just seeing old friends would be worth the effort.

Listed below are some more encouraging words and a few replies to some common concerns. Give a copy of this chapter to volunteers to read before they make their calls.

1.   Seeing former classmates, making new friendships and renewing old ones are perhaps the most common reasons

people attend their high school reunion. People who lost touch with former friends and acquaintances rediscover each other at reunions, during the planning process or just by phone. One friendship renewal occurred between two high school friends living on opposite coasts, neither of whom could attend the reunion.

> Having lost track of one another when they went separate ways after high school, Dava and Mary were reunited anyway. When Dava was contacted by the reunion committee, she was thrilled to learn the whereabouts of her former friend, Mary. While neither woman could attend the reunion, addresses were exchanged and they have been corresponding ever since.

2.   *"I don't want to come because no one I know will be there."* A common realization by reluctant alumni who go to their reunions after all is that they discover many classmates they forgot they knew.

One woman who attended her twentieth reunion complained afterward that she didn't see anyone she knew. A pre-reunion phone call or note from her probably would have brought some of her old friends. Have your alumni list available when making calls and encourage alumni to call and invite their old friends.

Remind alumni that everyone is an important part of their high school experience and that others would enjoy seeing them. Our reunion survey uncovered many responses that can attest to this fact.

3.   *"I probably don't have anything in common with anyone from high school anymore."* It is amazing how much we do have in common with people we haven't seen in many years, or may have little in common with and can still have a wonderful time. It might even be a boon for someone's business. A roofing specialist who attended his reunion

advertised his business card in the memory album and eventually received a lot of business from former classmates.

4. The reunion is an excellent opportunity to dispel old fears and haunting memories. After seeing old classmates as adults with the same responsibilities and problems as everyone else, old jealousies and fears will seem trivial and outdated. After all, most perspectives and maturity levels do change by adulthood.

> One alumni told a reunion committee caller that she resented the way she acted towards her in high school and accused her of being snobbish and conceited. Astonished by this reaction, the committee member apologized for her actions in high school, blamed them on her immaturity, and encouraged the woman to attend the reunion to allay her fears.

The happy ending to this story is that the woman attended the reunion and had a great time. She also apologized to the committee worker and thanked her for convincing her to attend. If people hold on to old intimidations and fears, they may find that reunions are the perfect opportunity to release them.

5. *"I didn't like who I was in high school. Why should I go and resurrect old discomforting feelings?"* After thoroughly enjoying her high school reunion, one author, who originally was repulsed at the thought of attending her reunion, wrote a book entitled *How To Survive Your High School Reunion . . . and Other Mid-life Crises.* She had some humorous, but poignant comments for reluctant high school reunion attendees:

> And it is predominately to this sector, haters of high school memories, that this is addressed. For I, too, grew squinty-eyed and suspicious about the emotional and behavioral backlash I'd suffer by re-exposing myself as an adult to that adolescent pecking order.

Ms. Markey proceeded to confess:

> To admit that I went, after years of oh-no-not-EVER speeches, is
> indeed humbling. But the next confession makes the preceding one
> benign. I HAD A WONDERFUL TIME. Beyond wonderful.

Ms. Markey then went on to illustrate several ways one
could overcome the reunion jitters and have a great time.

> I went to a class reunion that transcended fun and segued directly
> into the arena of emotional luminescence. And at the risk of
> sounding like some born-again nostalgia freak, I'm convinced that
> anyone who adheres to [the following] 11-point program not only
> will survive the damn reunion, but will be forced to admit it was an
> exceedingly terrific place to put in an appearance. [1]

6.   Without admitting this to anyone, many people will not
attend their reunion because they feel they were not popular
in high school. A woman who wrote a letter to *Dear Abby*
which appeared in the Los Angeles Times on March 31, 1989
said it aptly:

> DEAR ABBY: This is for all those people who don't want to go to
> their class reunions because they weren't popular--or didn't belong
> to the "in" crowd in high school and they thought no one would want
> to talk to them anyway. I didn't think anyone would talk to me
> either, but my husband and I decided to go to my 20th high school
> reunion. Abby, it was the best move we ever made. People were
> actually glad to see us! (We both graduated from the school, but in
> different years.) I hugged more people in two days than I had
> hugged in 20 years! I have never felt such a sense of love and
> belonging as I did at that reunion. There were no pretenses of
> where we came from since most of us came from working-class
> families; we came home to be together. I even made peace with an

---

[1] Judy Markey, *How To Survive Your High School Reunion ... and
Other Mid-life Crises,* (Chicago: Contemporary Books, 1984), 3-4.

old enemy! For those who organized that reunion in Pittsburgh, thank you from the bottom of my heart. For those who didn't make the effort to attend--you missed a wonderful weekend. [2]

7.   Impromptu post-reunion parties that usually occur can turn into all night "nostalgia sessions." These parties provide a cozy environment to continue reminiscing with small groups of friends.

Several of my old friends reminisced until 5 a.m. in my room at the hotel. It was great, we knew we would never again have such an opportunity to get together and talk like this.

"YOU'LL WONDER WHY YOU EVEN HESITATED"

According to an article in *Psychology Today*, a study based upon 482 surveys of reunion attendees was conducted by two psychologists on "Why People Go or Don't Go to Their High School Reunion." An interesting observation and conclusion was highlighted:

...the overwhelming majority of people had a marvelous time, despite initial apprehensions. More than 90 percent of our attendees would return again. So why not take the risk? The odds of having a good time are in your favor. [3]

The study suggests that once hesitant alumni get to their reunion, they will discover that reunions are really not so intimidating, will probably have a wonderful time and will

---

[2] Taken from a DEAR ABBY column by Abigail Van Buren. Copyright 1989 UNIVERSAL PRESS SYNDICATE. Reprinted with permission. All rights reserved.

[3] Douglas H. Lamb and Glenn D. Reeder, "Reliving Golden Days," *Psychology Today* (June 1986): 22-30.

not regret their decision to attend. They just need to give themselves the opportunity.

Before and After. If you can get reluctant alumni to attend their reunions, research shows they'll inevitably have a great time.

The article also revealed a common finding: that reunions "...mean renewing friendships, reminiscing with a small group of close friends and making comparisons with others. Perhaps more importantly, reunions appear to be catalysts for reflecting on our own lives and reaffirming our sense of belonging." [4]

We can all understand and appreciate these comments. You may have more ideas of your own to get alumni to attend. Good luck, try not to get discouraged and don't give up on anyone too easily.

---

[4] Lamb and Reeder, "Reliving Golden Days," 26.

NOTES

Chapter 4

Nine Months Before the Reunion

This is an appropriate time to send out the first reunion announcement. People will be wondering, at this point, if a reunion is being planned. In fact, your school already may be referring inquiries to you.

PREPARE THE FIRST MAILING

Getting the word out early gives you the opportunity of locating and notifying as many former classmates as possible. Over the past three months, hopefully volunteers have been providing updated alumni lists, so you should now have a substantial number of current addresses for the first mailing. If envelopes are being hand addressed or typed, and if there is enough time, ask volunteers to address the envelopes prior to the mailing meeting. If you are using labels, purchase a box of 100 sheets, preferably the ones that come with 33 labels per page.

Print alumni names and addresses on labels. Then print the committee's return address on labels to be affixed on the reply envelope.

The announcement goes to all alumni. Use whatever addresses are known, including the graduation address list provided by your school. For high school reunions, you will find that many parents still have the same address and can pass along reunion information to their children.

Include the statement **"Address Correction Requested"** somewhere on the outside of the envelope. The fee for this service is $.30 per address as of January 1992, but will be worth the savings in time and phone calls in trying to locate alumni who have moved.

Three benefits will be achieved from this early mailing:

- reservations with some early needed cash
- a collection of alumni histories for the memory album
- information on the whereabouts of other alumni

The mailer should contain the following items:

1. The Announcement

Design the invitation, using a computer with different fonts and graphics capabilities if you have access to one, to attract attention. (See sample invitations in Appendix A.) If you don't have a computer, get press-on letters available in most stationery stores. Print the announcement on colored paper, preferably in your school colors. If possible, include your high school logo or mascot. If you have the location of your reunion, give the date, location and time.

Create your own reunion announcements in your words and with your printer's available fonts. A questionnaire or survey for your classmates can also be formulated.

Cost per person/payment request. If you have a facility and know the cost per meal, you can create a preliminary budget (Chapter 2) and specify a ticket price. List a ticket price, even if you don't have a facility yet, by preparing a budget based on estimated costs. To encourage early reservations, designate cutoff dates for lower ticket prices and **describe how to make out the check.** "The Second Mailing" in Chapter 6 has sample payment schedules.

Payment acknowledgement. The announcement should indicate how ticket payments will be acknowledged, for example, "Your canceled check will be your receipt, and tickets will be held at the door." Or, "You will receive an acknowledgement postcard upon receipt of your check and tickets will be mailed to you approximately two weeks before the event."

Request the whereabouts of other classmates.

The reunion headquarter's address plus one or two reunion contact phone numbers.

Approximate date of next mailer. (Optional)

2. Reservation Form and Questionnaire

Some personal data is mandatory. Personal history questions are necessary only if you are presenting awards or are developing a survey.

Personal Data
- Alumni's Last Name, Maiden Name and First Name
- Number of Attendees
- Address, City, State and Zip Code
- Home and Business Phone
- Spouse or Guest's Name
- The location and/or phone number of someone who will always know your whereabouts

Personal History for Awards, Questionnaire or Survey
- If married, how long?
- How many children, grandchildren? Expecting date?
- Occupation.
- How far will you travel to attend the reunion?
- Did you marry your high school sweetheart?
- How close do you live to the high school?

Possible Memory Album Material
- Who were your favorite teachers from high school?
- What was your favorite song or musical group in school?
- What was the funniest/most memorable event in school?
- What are your hobbies?

One high school reunion committee included the question: "In high school I wanted to have a career as a _____ _____, I ended up a _____." The more interesting answers can be included in your memory album. (Chapter 5 offers other possible memory album contents.)

If you are incorporating alumni histories into your memory album, assign someone the task of editing and organizing the responses. Leave space on the questionnaire, or on the reverse of the response sheet. Ask alumni to briefly describe what has transpired in their lives since graduation.

One industrious twenty-five year reunion committee from an east coast high school compiled a list of public issue oriented questions and published the results in their memory album. Responses were entered into a computer database and the results were categorized and shown in percentages of the total class and by male and female responses. Occupation types, education levels and views on such issues as abortion, drugs and gun control were presented. It was a fascinating look on the alumni's new perspectives.

You can set up your own database to determine award winners or index responses from a survey. Enter your own categories. A sample survey appears in Appendix B.

Optional Requests

- *Enclose a business card and check for $_____ per card if you would like to advertise in the memory album.*
- *Can you donate a door prize?*
- *Can you volunteer on the committee?* Give suggestions for what is needed, e.g. mailing, phoning, slide show assistance, etc.
- *Would you be interested in purchasing a video of the reunion?* The cost will be approximately $_____.
- *What classmate would you most like to see at the reunion?* If you ask this question, try to utilize the answers constructively. In other words, during the phone drive you can say, "Dave Jones is hoping to see you there."
- *What teachers would you like to invite to the reunion?*
- *In what clubs, groups or activities did you participate in high school?* Code common groups such as the tennis team, drama club, chess club or swim team and make lists of attending members to display at the reunion.
- *Please send in a current family picture for a photo collage.*
- *Can you loan us any of your high school memorabilia, pictures or slides for display at the reunion?* (Requested slides could also be used in your slide show.) Be sure alumni identify their property if items are to be returned.
- *Would you like to make a donation to a scholarship (or gift) to be presented to the school?*

3. Other Enclosures

Response Label or Envelope. Make it as easy for alumni to respond by providing a pre-addressed return envelope or label. However, to keep postage costs down, make sure this insert does not cause the mailing to weigh over an ounce.

Missing Persons List. This page could wait to go out along with the second mailer, since the list will be shorter after responses arrive from the first mailing. It will get even shorter once additional updates come in from your committee members' researching efforts.

Items Needed for the Committee Mailing Meeting

Enlist volunteers to help affix labels, fold, stuff, stamp and seal the envelopes. Five or six people is a good start and you'll need the following items ready for the mailing:

1. **The reunion announcement.**

2. **Envelopes. Outer envelopes (#10)** with the reunion committee's name and address printed on the upper left hand corner of the envelopes. The recipient may be more likely to open or forward a reunion notification and not toss it out thinking it is junk mail.

If it does not make the mailer weigh over an ounce, include a **smaller return envelope (#9) or label.** When the reunion headquarters is selected, (usually someone's home) you will have the location for receiving payments.

3. **Rubber stamp.** To save on printing costs, purchase a rubber stamp with the reunion committee's name and address, and stamp the outer and return envelopes.

4. **Alumni address labels.**

5. **Postage.** First class stamps are preferable to bulk rate. The letter appears more personal and they are less likely to be thrown away. Also, acquiring a bulk rate permit requires cash, time and supervision and probably is not worth the savings in postage costs.

6. **Sponges** for stamping and sealing envelopes

PROVIDE ENTERTAINMENT

It is typical to have entertainment at reunions. Some additional ideas appear in Chapter 3 under "How To Portray an Enticing Reunion." However, this section discusses some of the more common forms of entertainment.

Musical Accompaniment

If you want live entertainment, it is a good idea to book your entertainer as soon as the reunion location is selected, especially if you hire a disc jockey who specializes in reunions. Here are a few suggestions:

-   A disc jockey (DJ) -- Depending upon how much your budget allows, and the involvement level you want, a DJ can be a "master of ceremonies" to spruce up your event, or someone who can just provide background music. The cost can range between $300 and $800.
-   A jukebox -- This can be very enjoyable. You can rent jukeboxes with music from any year and guests can select their own tunes.
-   Live band -- Be sure they can play the songs from the era you want and are a well established group. Also, be prepared for gaps of silence as they take rest breaks.
-   A tape deck playing continuous music -- If you have a smaller reunion, this option may fit your needs.

For more ideas or referrals on entertainers, ask other reunion committee members from your high school, catering managers of various hotels or friends who recently got married. Or, try the Yellow Pages under "Entertainers" or "Orchestras and Bands." Whatever musical entertainment you select, be sure to get references or better yet, try to see them perform in person.

Once the entertainment is lined up, be sure to discuss your musical preferences well in advance of your reunion. For example, you may want songs from a specific era or decade along with current musical arrangements. Also, tell the entertainer to keep the volume **low**. A common complaint at reunions is that background music is too loud to have conversations in the same room. Since talking is the predominant activity at reunions, having loud music can be very exasperating.

Special Events, Activities and Games

Some interesting and fun reunion activities were described in our survey of reunion goers. At one reunion, name tags were randomly given out to arriving guests. During the course of the evening each alumni had to find the person whose name tag he or she wore.

Another high school class was fortunate enough to boast a professional singer among their alumni. He entertained the alumni with a short performance of tunes popular during their high school era. At another reunion, sports teams and class officers were introduced, while at another reunion, approximately 100 past members of the high school class choir performed an impromptu concert. Another reunion had former cheerleaders lead some popular school cheers.

At a twenty-year reunion for San Gabriel High School in San Gabriel, California, someone from the local elementary school brought their group pictures taken in the first through sixth grades. Everyone who attended that same elementary school commingled in a separate area at the reunion and had a mini elementary school reunion.

Sometimes guests of alumni at reunions may feel out of place. Think of activities that would allow all guests to participate, such as having a dance contest or having the musician play music suitable for group dancing. This could be a good ice-breaker for the first dance after your program.

Video Tape

Videographers will tape your reunion. A reunion video will likely consist of an hour of candid shots of reunion activities and interviews of guests, all intertwined with background music. The video company may require a guarantee of sales, so be prepared to pay the minimum quota if there aren't enough sales at the reunion. You may not have a problem selling tapes at the reunion; however, to be certain, ask alumni in your mailings if they would be interested in buying one. The cost will be approximately $25 to $35 per tape.

If someone from your committee is knowledgeable and so inclined, he or she could make a video tape. Beginning with a tour of your school, the tape could contain interviews with former teachers and coaches. Then include footage from activities and highlights of the reunion dinner/dance. Set it up for display at the reunion and add the picnic activities later. Someone could take orders for the video at the reunion and have the appropriate number of copies made.

Slide Show

Another popular item at reunions is a slide show. Hiring a professional could be expensive, so check for prices and see if your budget will allow this expense. Again, a less costly version is to have a friend or committee member prepare a slide show. Photograph pictures from your school yearbook and make them into slides. Include pictures and slides donated by alumni and current shots of the school and surrounding familiar spots. Use a large screen (the hotel may have one) and have a one-time viewing, or set up a projector and smaller screen in another area for groups of people to watch during the course of the reunion. "The slide show was the highlight of the evening!" according to one alumni who attended his twenty-year high school reunion.

One reunion committee from Polytechnic High School in Sun Valley, California made such a slide show that played continuously throughout the evening. It included a tour of the high school grounds and former favorite hangouts. It also had interviews with former teachers as well as shots from their junior high and high school yearbooks.

Bring Yearbooks. It is fun and practical to bring yearbooks to your reunion. At a thirty-year reunion from Pasadena High School in California, attendees eagerly flipped through yearbooks that were brought. Many alumni had since lost their albums and not only relished the memories, but also were only able to remember former classmates from their pictures and inscriptions found inside the yearbooks.

HIRE THE PHOTOGRAPHER

There are a limited number of companies that specialize in reunion photography, so it is imperative to find one as soon as possible. In choosing a reunion photographer, ask to see a sample of their work. This book should contain the guests' pictures and an address directory. The photo album might include posed pictures of the evening's attendees as well as a collage page of candid shots. See if the photographer, family member or other volunteer can take black and white candid shots at the reunion for the collage page. The photo book should be included in your ticket price, however, if you want to keep your ticket price low, have someone sell orders for the books at the reunion.

One committee member from a high school in Long Beach, California was a printer. He prepared a professional hard-bound combination memory album/photo book. It contained candid pictures taken at the reunion dinner/dance and picnic and had almost 400 alumni histories. While this booklet was more expensive to produce than the memory album described in Chapter 5, part of the costs were absorbed by having alumni purchase advertising space with their business cards.

PLAN THE PICNIC

A picnic not only offers a chance for those who missed the main event to join in the reunion festivities, it also gives people more time to reminisce and catch those they missed at the dinner/dance. A picnic is also an opportunity for people to bring their families.

The Picnic. Families have fun at reunion picnics too!

A picnic could be held at a park near your school or even on the school grounds. Perhaps you could arrange for a tour of the school on the same day. If you choose a park, reserve the picnic areas and/or baseball diamond soon because you will be competing with Little Leagues and such for a prime weekend date. If you want to plan outdoor activities such as baseball, frisbee or soccer, request that alumni bring the relevant sports equipment.

The picnic time and location should be mentioned in all correspondence as soon as the details are known. Repeat the picnic particulars during the reunion and/or have a noticeable reminder at the registration tables or on the bulletin boards.

SET UP A BANK ACCOUNT

Open a reunion bank account when you receive several checks. For safety reasons you may want the names of two persons on the account with only one signature required to sign checks. Banking responsibilities include: making copies of checks, depositing them and keeping a record of all payments. The sample accounting ledger in Appendix C demonstrates one method for keeping track of your financial transactions.

More accounting guidelines and how to get various financial reports in the computer program begins on page 77.

Make Files. As you start accumulating large amounts of paper, buy legal size file folders and label them for identification. Files that could be categorized might include: "Committee Members," "Alumni Lists," "Contracts," "Reservations," "Copies of Checks," "Accounting Ledger (have some sort of enclosure for expense receipts)," "Business Cards for Advertisements," "Donations," "Phone Lists," "Announcements/Invitations" and "Media Ads."

Chapter 5

Six Months Before the Reunion

$\mathbf{B}$y this time you should have received several replies from the first mailing. A top priority should be to **update the alumni mailing list** with name and address changes. It is crucial to keep your alumni list current because if you start to lag behind, it could become difficult to catch up. You will also be severely limiting your attendance potential.

The essence of this chapter is based on the adage, "Don't put off 'til tomorrow what you can do today." Begin working on the tasks described in this chapter as soon as possible, otherwise, you might not have enough time to complete them and find you must eliminate one or more of them.

THE MEMORY ALBUM

In this book, the memory album represents a composite of alumni life stories. A short rendition of your classmates' activities since graduation is a great memento to hand out at the reunion or sold separately to those not able to attend. If you want to provide a memory album, here are some ideas for creating one:

- Request that someone from the committee alphabetize and edit the alumni histories.
- Place the autobiographies next to each alumni's yearbook picture. Leave the picture area blank if there is no yearbook picture, or use a current one, if available.
- Design a cover, title page and introduction page.

A memory album with a hard cover would be great to offer, but can be expensive. Talk to various printers and compare costs. The cover page should include the name of your school, the date of the reunion and graduation anniversary year. A picture of your school, mascot or other class insignia would contribute to the overall appearance. See Figure 5-1.

Figure 5-1. Sample class insignia

- The title page could include the reunion date and place as well as the names of committee members. The introduction page could be a statement from committee members welcoming the class to the reunion.

- Additional pages could include responses from your questionnaire, such as memorable or humorous high school moments, or a consensus on the findings on your most popular teacher, song or musical group. One memory album for a twenty-year reunion had three pages of references to fads, movies, books and national events which were popular during their graduation year.

- Include pictures from the school yearbook or current pictures of the school or other popular site.

- An "In Memorial" page

- If you prepared a database of responses to your questionnaire like the one described on page 60, list the survey results.

- An advertisement page with business cards of alumni or other establishment

Once the design and content of your memory album is finalized, check with several printers and compare prices. To reduce the cost, ask your former high school print shop to prepare it as a class project. If you go this route, pay close attention and monitor the progress very carefully, high school students may not be as careful as a professional printer.

NAME TAGS

Name tags are a MUST at any reunion. If you are making your own name tags and are ambitious, start preparing them for those people who have mailed in their ticket money; otherwise, wait until closer to the event and do them all at once. It is highly desirable to include the yearbook pictures on the name tags. Not only do the tags identify the guests, they can also stimulate introductions and conversations and serve as payment confirmation. Guests without name tags could be targeted for payment. Some name tag suggestions include:

- Button pins with names and yearbook pictures. These are very nice souvenirs, but expensive. Ask your printer or local stationery store for referrals, or look in the Yellow Pages under "Buttons."

•   Create your own name tags.   Photocopy yearbook pictures on a good copier. A printer can make copies for you on one of their better machines. Also, you might want to have the pictures slightly enlarged for greater visibility (especially helpful for twenty-five year and above reunions).   Have someone who is good at calligraphy write the names on the tags or have the names typed on. Then use a glue stick or rubber cement to attach the pictures onto the tags. See Figure 5-2.

Figure 5-2. Sample name tag

Buy the clear plastic pin name tags sold in most stationery or office supply stores.

The computer program can print your name tags on the suggested paper described in the User's Guide.

If you don't want to involve pins, glue the pictures onto self-adhesive paper or tags and laminate them. Use velcro strips or other adhesive to be affixed on the guests' clothing.

Whatever approach you use, it is recommended that name tags be prepared in advance and not left for arriving guests to fill out on their own.

Use only the maiden names of female alumni on the name tags or include both maiden and married names. If both names are used, underline or highlight the maiden name. Guests of alumni should also have name tags. Their tags can have the name only, or their name accompanied with the saying: "Quit staring, I'm only a guest."

THE SECOND MAILING

As you prepare for the second mailing, make sure your alumni list is updated with current name and addresses. The second mailing will be more specific with information on the reunion. If you didn't mention it in the first mailing, request that alumni pay for their tickets now.

Items to be Included in the Mailing

1.   **The Announcement.**   Similar to the first one, the announcement should include any new information that was not available before, such as date, time and place for the event and the picnic. Resend the questionnaire form and/or survey to whose who have not responded to the first mailing. This may be to the entire class again if only a few alumni responded so far; and early respondents won't mind getting another announcement.

If you are working with professional planners, be sure to insist that picnic details are included in all announcements. They may be reluctant to advertise the picnic since their fees are usually only a result of ticket sales.

Payment Request. If you haven't already requested money for ticket purchases, do so in this mailing. Set one or more early payment deadlines with the lowest ticket price as your base price to encourage early responses. Request the highest price for tickets purchased at the door. A sample payment schedule might look like this for a June 10th reunion date:

By April 30th .....$40.00 per person, $75.00 per couple
By May 31st ....$45.00 per person. $85.00 per couple
At the door ....$50.00 per person, $95.00 per couple

or, with only one price break:

Before May 1st ....$45.00 per person
May 2nd and after........ $55.00 per person

While it is not usually done, some reunion committees may offer refunds. If you do, stipulate that ticket payments only be refunded until a specified date. It is rare that people request refunds.

2.   Alphabetized list of missing classmates

Indicate all those alumni with known addresses as "Found." Also mark as found all those who responded, as well as those who are deceased. Then print the list of all alumni not found.

3. **Hotel flyer or information on accommodations.** If the reunion is at a hotel, or there is one nearby and you were able to work out a discount room rate, see if they have a small flyer to include in your mailing, light enough to keep the mailing under 1 ounce. If this makes the mailing too heavy, just include hotel information along with the group discount room rate in your announcement. You can usually negotiate a discounted room rate for large groups.

4. **Address labels and envelopes.** Buy envelopes and labels. As in the first mailing, buy the #10 envelopes and imprint your return address on the envelopes. Take out names in your alumni list that were returned from your first mailing so another label will not be addressed or generated from your computer until the correct address is known.

Print addresses on labels or directly on the envelopes. Print the reunion headquarter's address on labels or envelopes if you are including a reply envelope. Labels will be generated for all alumni listed as "found."

5. **Return envelopes or labels.** Use the smaller (#9) envelopes or labels with the committee's pre-printed return address. These are good for encouraging responses.

6. **Postage.** In order to calculate the necessary first class postage, take your class size and exclude classmates who already paid and those whose letters were returned from the first mailing with no new address.

7. **Sponges** for stamping and sealing envelopes.

TICKETS AND ACKNOWLEDGEMENTS

Tickets are an added cost to produce and mail, but can serve as a nice memento. The reception process will be much less complicated if your guests arrive with tickets in hand. And, the reception desk workers will have a paid reservation list handy, in case someone forgets their tickets.

If you want to design your own tickets, prepare them now. Copy or draw a picture of your school's mascot or class emblem, or take a picture of your school's main entrance or other familiar spot as a background for the reunion particulars. Include a serrated ticket stub for the door prize drawing. See the sample custom ticket in Figure 5-3.

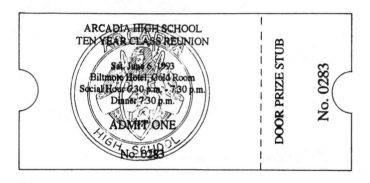

Figure 5-3. Sample "do it yourself" ticket. Design the tickets to be both a practical item and a souvenir.

A less costly method would be to use "movie-type" ticket stubs to be given to each guest in the reception packets. These are available at most party or stationery stores. The double rolls have two tickets connected to each other with the same number. One ticket stub is retained for the door prize drawing and the guest keeps the other.

If you do not send out tickets, indicate on the announcement something like: *"Your canceled check is your receipt. Tickets will be held at the door."* It is possible to forego tickets altogether. The registration packets (Chapter 9) can serve as the "tickets" and the name tags can act as payment vouchers at the reunion. The reservation or attendance list (Chapter 8) is an added verification of payment.

Acknowledgements

Record and acknowledge payments promptly. The bulk of the ticket money will usually arrive by the deadline with the lowest ticket price, and again just before the reunion as people will wait until the last minute to pay or to decide whether or not to attend. Mention in your mailers how ticket payments will be handled so when alumni send in their money, they will know what to expect.

Acknowledgement Postcards. Respondents who mailed in their money need some confirmation that their check was received. A postcard acknowledgement is relatively inexpensive and easy. Purchase blank postcards and have a general receipt message printed on them. Include the date, time and place of the reunion and the number of tickets they purchased. In addition, reiterate how and if tickets will be involved (see Figure 5-4).

Accounting Guidelines for Ticket Purchases

Indicate on your accounting ledger, those alumni that paid. (See example in Appendix C.) If you are using index cards, highlight the paid purchasers with some sort of noticeable mark or colorful sticker. Make copies of all checks before depositing them in the bank. This essential backup is your double-check for all payments.

Enter payments in the Guest/Budget Data section of the program. The program can print all payments above a particular amount in order to segregate the ticket payments from the item purchases.

Write the letters AC for "Acknowledgement Postcard Sent" on the copies of deposited checks as your verification that one was sent.

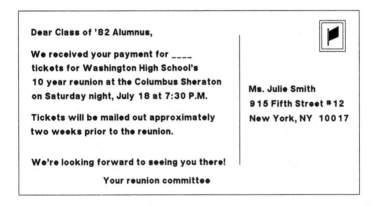

Dear Class of '82 Alumnus,

We received your payment for ____ tickets for Washington High School's 10 year reunion at the Columbus Sheraton on Saturday night, July 18 at 7:30 P.M.

Tickets will be mailed out approximately two weeks prior to the reunion.

We're looking forward to seeing you there!

Your reunion committee

Ms. Julie Smith
915 Fifth Street #12
New York, NY 10017

Figure 5-4. Sample postcard acknowledgement

Chapter 6

Three Months Before the Reunion

There are only ninety days before the reunion, so you should use the time judiciously. Begin by editing the incoming alumni histories for your memory album, and make any necessary corrections to your alumni address list.

The emphasis at this juncture is on increasing attendance through a phone drive and media advertisements; organizing the decorations; and arranging for the reception desk workers.

THE PHONE DRIVE

To achieve a higher turnout, make phone contact with as many alumni as possible. Making personal telephone calls to people should boost your attendance immensely by motivating those who procrastinate or are indecisive, or who may have misplaced their reunion information. Another significant effect of the phone drive is that it may produce further information on alumni still not located.

Due to the successful efforts of committee members in locating alumni, you should have a sizable list of telephone

numbers by now. Remind committee members to ask for
referral information on the whereabouts of other alumni.

Select the option for printing the phone
list and divide it among the volunteers.
The lists can be sequenced by area codes
so people do not have to make long distance
calls. A column for comments is included.

**A lot of your volunteer work on the phone bank can be accomplished at
home.**

In organizing the phone bank, try to reserve one evening
every week for making calls. Even if just two or three
people can meet and call from someone's office or home, the
time will be well spent. If one phone location is not feasible,
split up the phone lists between committee members. Ask
callers to be responsible for giving any "new" information
(address, phone or name changes) to the person in charge of
the alumni records or computer list.

Include a column for comments on your phone list for
committee members to record remarks from their calls.

These comments will be very helpful for general information and when organizing future phone drives.

MEDIA ANNOUNCEMENTS

Place ads announcing the reunion. Send notices to local newspapers and radio stations. Reunion announcements are usually free of charge because they are considered public service announcements. Contact your local newspapers and radio stations to find out if they handle reunion announcements and to obtain their procedures and formats for sending them information. Provide the essential details: School name, graduation year and reunion anniversary; date of reunion; contact person and phone number. Follow up by calling the newspaper or radio station.

Suggestion: Send your school a copy of one of your newspaper ads.

DECORATIONS, DISPLAYS AND OTHER MEMENTOS

Table Decorations. Refer to your budget to determine how much was allocated for table centerpieces. Then come up with various ideas for centerpieces. Some suggestions are listed below:

• Floral arrangements can very affordable. If you want fresh flowers for centerpieces and the reunion is in May or June, make your selections early, because these months are the busiest in the floral industry. The hotel or restaurant sponsoring your reunion may have a list of florists that you could use. Compare prices.

• Helium balloons attached to some decorative centerpiece are festive and attractive. Helium balloons can be delivered by companies that specialize in balloon designs, or a helium tank can be rented, and balloons can be blown up just prior to the reunion. You will need **at least** four or five people and several hours on reunion day to inflate the balloons, so, consider the time you have available to decorate when deciding on the room decor. Five latex balloons in your school colors per table will be very festive. For variety, you could use four latex balloons and one larger mylar balloon on some tables.

Try not to overinflate each balloon, because you could run out of helium before all the balloons are filled. Here is what happened to one reunion committee.

> After blowing up only 80 of 100 balloons, all the helium was used up. A frantic call was made to a committee member on her way to the reunion. She was asked to purchase and bring twenty more inflated balloons. It was fortuitous the party supply store was still open and all the balloons could fit in her car.

• A centerpiece could be created around the theme of your reunion or other high school memento.

Tie centerpieces to a theme. They should be eye catching and colorful.

Suggestion: There might be some unique memento from your high school that could be used for centerpieces or as award presentations. For example, a twenty-five year reunion for Los Angeles High School got bricks from the tower of their original school building after it was destroyed by an earthquake. These bricks were used as table centerpieces at the reunion and also presented as plaques during their awards ceremony.

• Inexpensive wicker baskets can be filled with tissue paper in your school colors. Helium balloons can emanate from the baskets. Make copies of various high school documents such as your diploma, the graduation program, yearbook pictures, etc. Have them laminated and attached to sturdy sticks. Scatter colorful confetti (school colors, perhaps) around the table.

• A bottle of wine with the school's name, class year and reunion date printed on the label can be quite pretty with balloons and colorful ribbons tied to the bottlenecks. These could also serve as door prizes. A winery in California, Windsor Vineyards, produces excellent bottled wines with your own inscription on the labels. They can be reached at (800)289-9463.

Banner. A reunion banner can be a spirited welcome to reunion guests. The banner can also be used at the picnic and for future reunions if you get one that is durable. A sizable vinyl sign can be purchased for approximately $100.00. Check with some local sign companies in the Yellow Pages under "Signs" and call for prices. Computer produced signs are considerably less expensive but they will only last for one evening.

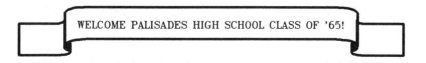

Figure 6-1. Sample banner

T-shirts, Sweatshirts and Golf Shirts. Popular items to offer for sale at your reunion are T-shirts, sweatshirts and/or golf shirts. Many reunion photographers and other specialists can prepare T-shirts in your school colors with your school name and the last two numbers of your graduation year imprinted on the front. The numbers are filled in with the full names of all alumni.

Reunion T-shirts do not cost your committee any money. The vendor will make the T-shirts and offer them for sale at your reunion. If the supply of T-shirts is exhausted at the reunion, orders will be taken and the shirts mailed to alumni. It is very profitable for the vendors, popular at reunions and virtually no work for the reunion committee.

Nostalgia Table. Have a display of school memorabilia on a "nostalgia table" with such items as letterman sweaters, school newspapers, regulation booklets, graduation program or other school mementos. Some items such as letters received from classmates unable to attend can be posted on bulletin boards provided by the hotel.

Picture Blowups. Old pictures or posters reminiscent of your school days are great for reunions. Some suggestions:

- Year book or personal pictures blown up to poster size
- Movie posters popular during your school years. A store in Hollywood, California sells movie posters. Depending upon the poster, the cost can range between $10 and $100. Hollywood Movie Posters: (213)463-1792
- Senior class group photo enlarged
- Enlarged front pages of newspapers from your graduation year

> One twenty-year class reunion committee member from Sun Valley, California had photos and stories from his junior and high school newspapers blown up for display at his reunion.

Napkins. Cocktail napkins in school colors imprinted with your school's name, date of reunion and graduation year are festive and inexpensive favors. Most party supply or stationery stores can order these for you.

"In Memorial." A display of known deceased alumni with their yearbook pictures is always a thoughtful tribute to former classmates.

Picture Collage. If you requested family pictures of alumni, prepare a "picture collage" in a framed display.

RECEPTION DESK WORKERS

Organize reception desk workers. It helps to have capable and enthusiastic people sitting at the registration tables. Their responsibilities include checking people in, handing out registration packets and memory books, collecting payments and directing arrivals to the photographer. Committee members could assume these roles; however, if they prefer not to, perhaps friends, co-workers or family members could help out.

Committee members get to greet everyone first.

Try to enlist at least five or six people to work at the reception tables. By reunion time, if it turns out only three or four people are available to help, you will meet the minimum requirement. Two to three people are needed to hand out reception packets and at least one person must handle the will-call table for those guests paying at the door. **Someone from the committee should remain near the reception tables welcoming guests and supervising during the entire registration process.**

> At one reunion, the ten year old sons of two of the committee members wore their fathers' original high school letterman sweaters and stood outside the door to greet the guests.

See Chapter 9 for details on the contents of the registration packets and specific responsibilities for each reception desk worker.

THE COUNTDOWN

7	One Month Before the Reunion	89
8	Two Weeks Before the Reunion	97
9	One Week Before the Reunion	101

Chapter 7

One Month Before the Reunion

Continue with the phone drive and editing the alumni histories during this last month before the reunion. With the majority of your reunion plan accomplished at this point, you will be pleased to discover that there are only a few details remaining. Volunteer help is crucial, so ask committee members for help with these final tasks.

REMINDER NOTICES

Postcard reminder notices should be sent out at this point. A printer can make them in one day. Send the reminder notices to any alumni not heard from that you have valid addresses for. These reminder notices should encourage lackadaisical alumni to take action. See Figure 7-1.

MAKE NAME TAGS

Hopefully, the phone drive has been successful and is continuing. Even this close to the event, there may be some alumni who still have not heard about the reunion. By now, however, you should have a substantial list of paid guests and potential attendees. Create a list of alumni who bought tickets, or pull out the marked index cards from your card file representing paid alumni and start making name tags. To save time later, make name tags for those alumni who indicated probable attendance as well.

Print a list of paid alumni and their guests from the program and then either type or print the names onto tags. You could also print the names directly from the program onto the tags.

It is not uncommon to receive an influx of ticket payments only a few days before the reunion, so try to prepare as many name tags as you can now. Only one last committee meeting may be all that's necessary to complete the name tags and prepare the registration packets. See Chapter 9 for an explanation of the registration packets.

Figure 7-1. Sample postcard reminder notice.

THE PROGRAM

The Printed Program

A printed program of the evening's events is a nice souvenir. It could be one sheet of thick paper stock folded over with your school logo on the cover along with the name, date and place of the reunion and picnic. See Figure 7-2. The inside might have an approximate time frame for the evening's activities. If a program is the only item you are handing out, you could include extra pages with some of the memory album material suggested on pages 69-71 such as: expressions of appreciation and names of reunion committee members and other volunteers for their efforts; a welcome to invited guests; acknowledgements to donors of door prizes and awards; or, results of any alumni survey (see sample survey in Appendix B).

Figure 7-2. One version of a reunion program

The Spoken Program

An important part of the evening, typically right after dinner and during dessert, is the program. It may be the one time during the evening when one activity has everyone's attention. Some reunion committees prefer not to have any program. However, some sort of program is usually planned at most reunions, if only to make short announcements about the picnic, to present awards and presentations or to introduce special guests.

The key word here is short. Talking should be held to a maximum of 20 minutes. Speeches are **not** recommended, they can be disastrous and boring. Keep any dialogue short, punchy and focused. If you have a slide show, video or other visual portion of your program, keep that at a minimum too. The main activity of the evening is reminiscing.

Your DJ or band leader can assist you in acting as a master of ceremonies. Discuss this responsibility with the entertainer. If you are renting a jukebox, or prefer to handle the program on your own, make sure you have a podium and microphone. The hotel or restaurant will usually provide these items at no additional cost.

Create a rough draft of program notes. When you have the final draft completed, give a copy to each participating person with their section highlighted. See Figure 7-3.

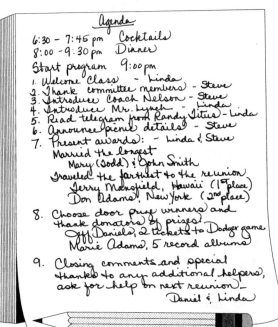

Figure 7-3. Sample personal program notes to be read at the podium.

Announcements. These could include details on the picnic or other related events; a reminder to take pictures; a request to purchase raffle tickets (if your bank account needs help); assistance on the next reunion; a plea for people to send in address changes for future reunions; or a reading of any special letters or telegrams.

Acknowledgements, Introductions and Presentations. Thank anyone who contributed to the planning of the reunion, and any donors of door or award prizes. Introduce any special guests, and present any plaques or commemorations. Try to get a camera-toting volunteer to take a picture of any special presentation for inclusion in the photo album's collage page.

Awards. Past a certain age group, awards for married longest, etc. cease to be interesting. However, they are quite popular up through and including twenty-year reunions.

If you are planning to give away awards and/or door prizes, prepare a preliminary program now. Reread the alumni histories and choose tentative award winners. As questionnaires still come in, winners of these awards may need to be revised.

- Married the Longest
- Most Recently Married
- Traveled the Farthest to the Reunion
- Lives Closest to the High School
- Still Married to Their High School Sweetheart
- Most Children, Grandchildren
- Nearest to Being a Parent
- Nearest to Being a Grandparent
- Most Unique Occupation
- Changed the Least Since High School (This prize will be decided on the evening of the event with nominations during the program.)

You may come up with different categories, but please, keep them tactful. Don't award a prize for "the least hair," "changed the most" or "married the most." The winner would probably not appreciate such recognition.

Door prizes. Select ticket stubs for door prize winners.

DOOR PRIZES AND AWARDS

If anyone responded to your questionnaire volunteering to provide prizes for goods or services, call them and graciously acknowledge their generous donation. If appropriate, verify that the item will be brought to the reunion, or make arrangements for it to be picked up. If door prizes are in the form of services, describe them on nicely designed coupons (see Figure 7-4).

∞ **Gift Certificate** ∞

for:

Two Tickets any Thursday Evening

For The Hollywood Bowl - Summer Season 1992

( )

Donated By   **Phone**

∴ **Gift Certificate** ∴

This Certificate entitles: *The Bearer*

To: *Any Selection of Books*

Call: *Hiliary/Walden Books*   **At:** *(310) 555-4321*

Donated by: *Diane Jones*   **Value:** *$50.00*

Figure 7-4. Sample coupons of donated services to present to award winners

If you need to purchase door prizes, do so now. They don't have to be expensive; a creative memento will be appreciated and remembered. If you aren't using tickets, purchase the double stubbed "movie tickets" available in most party stores with matching numbers for use in selecting door prize winners.

SET UP THE DECORATIONS

Decorations and displays take forethought, people power and reliance on your time management skills. Depending on how early you can have the banquet room, your ability to put up elaborate decorations on the day of your reunion may be limited. Consider the time and energy it will take to decorate, and plan accordingly.

If someone in your committee or a family friend has some artistic talent, solicit his or her help in creating some signs for specified areas at the reunion. Some signs could include a drawing of the school mascot. Possible signs might be:

- *Welcome University High Chieftains Class of '79*
- *Registration*
- *Pre-paid Guests*
- *Will Call Tickets*
- *Late Registration Can Purchase Tickets Here*
- *Photo Line Starts Here* or *Purchase Photos Here*
- *Buy Reunion T-Shirts Here*
- *Trip for Two to Hawaii! Buy Your Raffle Tickets Here*
- *Purchase Drink Tickets Here*

Any displays, banner or wall hangings will have to be removed at the end of the evening. Table centerpieces can be taken home, but someone from the committee should be responsible for collecting all other decorations and memorabilia. **A dependable person should be in charge of**

the safekeeping of the cash box. If you are spending the night at the hotel, ask the hotel to lock your cash box in their safe deposit box overnight.

PHOTOGRAPHER CARDS

The photographer will likely request completed identification cards before the reunion. Depending on your preference, these identification cards can either be mailed out to alumni to be completed and brought to the reunion, or cards could be typed up by a volunteer and placed inside the registration packets. Ask arriving alumni to verify the information on the cards as the packets are handed out. The photographer may ask you to confirm the addresses anyway, but errors might be more easily noticed by arriving alumni.

Chapter 8

Two Weeks Before the Reunion

As you head down the stretch toward the finish line, don't get too focused on the winning post. There are some important sideline activities in the guise of loose ends. Updating the guest list and finalizing the handouts and other displays could be overlooked in these final weeks as your attention becomes concentrated on the registration process. You can get started on the registration packets now. The procedures are described in Chapter 9.

THE ATTENDANCE LIST

You should have a sizable attendance list by now. Prepare a preliminary list of paid guests and include alumni name, number in party and amount paid. This list will be very useful to the reception desk workers. If you have a computer, this task will be easy. On the other hand, if you must create this list, use a pencil (there may be changes) and go over the final guest list in black ink for readability. Some ticket payments will still trickle in at the last minute; hence, a final update should be prepared the day before the reunion.

The computer program will print your attendance list. It will include the name, number in party and amount paid for all alumni who bought tickets.

LOOSE ENDS

A few reminders: any hand-made signs, decorations or table centerpieces should be in the final stages of completion. Pick up donated awards or remind donors who are bringing their prizes. Have an extra bottle of wine just in case someone forgets to bring their donation.

Verify the attendance of your reception desk workers, check on floral arrangements or prepare your own table centerpieces. Call entertainer, videographer, photographer, T-shirt and other vendors to confirm time of arrival. Finally, confirm the attendance of invited guests and make arrangements for their hotel rooms. If your budget allows this, offer to pay for their room if they are arriving from out of town.

Finalize Program Announcements and Award Winners

Update your program notes with any changes in award winners for those questionnaires still arriving. This should be the deadline for making changes. Any other corrections in your current selection of winners will have to wait until the next reunion.

Memory Albums, Handouts and Displays

Deliver the camera-ready draft of the memory album, program or other handout to your printer. Make sure you have sufficient time to proofread the printer's draft and be able to receive the final product at least three days before the event. Waiting until this late enables you to include any alumni histories into the memory album that may arrive at the last minute. **PLEASE allow several hours for final proofreading. Check the spelling of names and make sure the alumni descriptions match the correct person.** Here is what happened to one reunion committee:

> A high school print shop teacher was hired to print the memory albums. Either as a mistake or intentionally, someone working on the project placed the occupation (a belly dancer) of one alumni next to the picture of another student who became a concert violinist. This alteration was not noticed until all the albums were distributed.

The banner, posters and any other prizes should be in hand by now. If you are having a slide show presentation, go through at least one rehearsal to verify that the slides are in good order and the program is kept within your allowed time slot. (Remember, the entire program should not last more that twenty minutes.)

MAIL THE TICKETS

Do not wait later than two weeks before the reunion to mail out your tickets. Because the U.S. Mail system is so unpredictable, do not take the risk of alumni not receiving their tickets before the reunion. If you are using bulk rate mail, and we suggest that you don't, allow a month for delivery. This mode of mail service has been known to take up to a month or longer to reach their destinations.

Print address labels for all paid guests. Check the computer program User's Manual for the recommended label size for your printer.

When sending out tickets, you may want to include a short note with information on the picnic and/or other reunion events. This note can also go to alumni who responded that they would not be attending the main event. Who knows, someone may decide to attend a related event at the last moment.

Last Minute Cash Flow Problems?

Remember, it will probably not be well received to ask alumni to donate to a reunion fund at the reunion. Hopefully, you budgeted well and expenses have not exceeded revenues. However, in the event you are running short, refer to some of the suggestions described in Chapter 2, pages 43-44 for help in raising last minute cash.

Chapter 9

One Week Before the Reunion

Countdown . . . Feeling relieved that reunion day is fast approaching, you might also be experiencing a little anxiety. If you have been following the instructions in this book, however, you should be well organized.

REGISTRATION

After updating your alumni list with any last minute ticket purchases, prepare a final attendance list. Purchase envelopes for the registration packets. Depending upon the size of your name tags, the largest enclosure will likely be the photo card, therefore the small 4 x 7 envelopes available in most grocery stores (they come 100 to a box) should be adequate. With three or four people helping, your committee can fill the registration packets in one evening.

Before the final meeting and using the attendance list as a guide, write or type the alumni's name, guest name and the number of paid tickets on the outside of each envelope.

The registration packets should contain the following items:

Name Tags. As described in Chapter 5, name tags should include the maiden and married names of female alumni. Be sure to include name tags for the guests of alumni too.

Suggestion: Prepare extra registration packets with name tags and photo cards for those alumni who didn't pay, but indicated they might attend (to be held at the Will Call table). It won't take that much extra effort and the packets will be ready when and if the alumni arrives.

Photo cards. These cards should be completed according to your photographer's directions.

Tickets. Tickets will only be included in those registration envelopes for alumni who paid for their tickets too late to have them mailed.

Will Call

It will be much less complicated to have the Will Call transactions handled at a separate table from the prepaid registration area. Cash settlements take longer, and it is best to have the person handling cash concentrate on only one activity. For those alumni who indicated they would be paying at the door, highlight the phrase *"Balance Due - $_____ "* in red on the envelope, see Figure 9-1. This conspicuous reminder alerts the person collecting payments to get a check for the amount indicated.

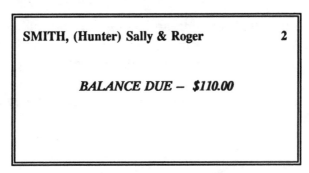

SMITH, (Hunter) Sally & Roger   2

BALANCE DUE – $110.00

Figure 9-1. Sample Registration Packet Inscription

When unannounced alumni show up at the door, place their payment inside an envelope and write their name on the envelope. **It is especially important to identify those guests who pay for their tickets with cash.** Having unidentified cash payments can be very frustrating later on.

Reception Desk Items

The following items are needed at the reception tables:

1. Registration packets
2. Alphabetical list of all paid reunion attendees with amounts paid
3. List of Will Call ticket holders
4. Memory albums and/or other hand outs
5. Large block letters, representing the first letters of last names of alumni to limit confusion and long lines at the registration tables. If 200 or more people are attending, form at least three lines. The ability to have three lines depends, of course, on the number of people working the reception tables. A group of letters might look like this:

A - H   I - P   Q - Z

Suggestion: Prepare large signs identifying the pre-paid and Will Call ticket areas. The facility may have stands available to display these signs behind each table.

6. Blank name tags
7. Pens, pencils, blank envelopes, tape
8. Cash box for the Will Call table, and some bills in change such as $1's, $5's and $10's for last minute arrivals
9. Container for door prize ticket stubs; better yet, ask the restaurant/hotel for a one.

Reception Desk Workers' Responsibilities

To facilitate an orderly reception process, designate assignments for each worker. Ask your spouse or guest to help out if you don't have enough volunteers or paid workers. If alumni are helping out at the tables, have relief people take over after the first hour. Family members, friends or paid workers can take breaks once the reception period is over. But try to have the desks manned for most of the evening for late arrivals and to monitor those who may stroll in. **Alumni who arrive after dinner should be charged a portion of the ticket price to help cover all the other costs associated with the reunion.**

Will Call Table. One person can be in charge of the Will Call table for those guests paying at the door. Responsibilities will include handling ticket transactions, making name tags and tearing off any door prize ticket stubs. Memory albums or other handouts should also be available at this table. **The cash box should always be under supervision or in a safe place.**

Pre-paid Ticket Holders. A minimum of two people (three would be best) are needed to process arrivals. In addition to greeting alumni, they will do the following:

• Hand out registration packets.
• Hand out memory album, program or other prepared booklet. (You could place programs on a separate table at the entrance or at each place setting.)
• Ask alumni to verify the addresses on their photo cards.
• Direct guests toward the photographer to have their pictures taken. (The photographer will make sure pictures are taken without name tags.)
• If ticket stubs are used for door prizes, tear off stubs.

FINAL ARRANGEMENTS WITH THE FACILITY OR CATERER

The Meal Count

The restaurant or caterer will require a meal count guarantee and may even want 90 percent to full payment a week in advance of the event. With your paid list, plus a few extra who promised to pay at the door, you should have a number to give the facility. Most restaurant facilities should be able to accommodate up to a 7 percent overage of your guarantee (check with your facility) to allow for unexpected guests. Don't overestimate the number of potential attendees, because the few unannounced arrivals will be balanced by the inevitable no-shows. Refunds are not usually requested or for that matter ever offered. Time, effort and additional cost factors more than compensate for paid no-shows.

Items Available Through the Facility

If you need any of the following items, confirm availability with the facility.

1. Reception tables
2. Stands for holding letters or signs
3. Easels and/or bulletin boards for posters, pictures and other displays
4. Podium and microphone
5. A place to hang your banner in the banquet hall
6. Screen for slide show
7. Television and video monitor
8. Container for door prize ticket stubs

CONTINGENCY PLAN

It would be smart to have a back-up contingency plan in case a key person in charge is unable to attend the reunion. At least one other person should be aware of the evening's responsibilities and prepared to take over.

REUNION DAY AND AFTERWARDS

| 10 | The Reunion Event | 109 |
| 11 | After the Reunion | 115 |

Chapter 10

The Reunion Event

The Big Day! In just a few hours your reunion will occur. This chapter provides a scenario and an approximate time schedule on how your reunion day activities might unfold.

AT HOME

9:00 a.m. -- Begin the day

Call the hotel or restaurant to verify how soon you can enter the banquet room to start setting up. Try to give yourselves several hours in advance of the reunion to prepare the room. Bring your reunion attire to change into later. If you have a complementary room, committee workers can change there. If the reunion event is not at a hotel, leave yourself plenty of time to return home to change clothes, or better yet, use someone's home who lives nearby.

Copy the checklist below of reunion day supplies and check off those items as you gather them. The blank space can be filled with something we left out.

Reunion Day Necessities

	ITEMS TO BRING		TO DO
	Memory Albums and/or Programs		Call facility. When can you start setting up?
	Registration Packets		Set up table centerpieces
	Cash Box with some dollars in change		Arrange registration packets
	List of Paid Guests		Hang banner, etc.
	Memorabilia: photo collage, nostalgia items, other displays		Meet and explain responsibilities to reception desk workers
	Extra Tickets		Meet with photographer
	Blank Name Tags		Meet with DJ or performer
	Stapler, Scotch Tape		Meet with maitre d'
	Pens and Pencils		Meet with T-shirt vendor
	Banner		Get dressed
	Posters, other room decor		
	Table Centerpieces		
	Door Prizes		
	Award Prizes or Coupons		
	Checkbook		
	Personal Program Notes		
	Letter Designations for Guest Reception Area		
	Clothes for the Reunion		
	Camera (if you are taking your own candid shots)		

Optional or As Necessary

___ Easels/Bulletin Boards. (Only if the facility doesn't provide them)
___ Slide Show Equipment
___ Video Tape Equipment

AT THE FACILITY

1:00 p.m. -- Set up the room

- Set up table centerpieces, posters, decorations and other memorabilia.

- Organize the reception tables with registration packets in alphabetical order.

- Hang the banner.

5:00 p.m. -- Get ready

- Get dressed.
- Take a breath.

5:45 p.m. -- Coordinate the evening's agenda

- Greet and discuss the evening's agenda with committee members, photographer, entertainer and maitre d'.

- Coordinate with the entertainer if and when they will act as master of ceremonies or make any introductions. Remind the entertainer to consider the guests and keep the music at a low volume. (After all, this is your reunion, so don't be afraid to insist on this.)

- Find out how late the photographer will be at the reunion to take pictures.

- Go over the responsibilities of each reception desk worker.

THE REUNION

6:30 - 7:30 p.m. -- Social Hour

Someone from the reunion committee should supervise the registration process and make sure the cash box is in a safe place at all times.

8:00 - 9:30 p.m. -- Dinner

The Big Night. A time for friendship, food and fun

9:00 - 9:30 p.m -- Program (Refer to your notes)

- Welcome alumni
- Thank committee members
- Introduce special guests
- Present slide show
- Make announcements
- Present awards
- Select door prize winners
- Give picnic details, request sports equipment
- Request volunteers for the next reunion
- Closing comments

9:30 - ? -- Dancing and reminiscing

BEFORE LEAVING THE EVENT

Retrieve the cash box, banner, and all registration supplies before leaving the event.

THE PICNIC

The picnic offers a chance for alumni to bring their families and to continue reminiscing. Also, many of those who were unable to attend the dinner/dance will have the chance to visit at the picnic.

Since people will be bringing their own lunch, all you have to think about bringing is:

- Your lunch and any sports equipment

- The reunion banner for display in your picnic area

- Extra memory books for picnic attendees who may want to buy them. Programs for souvenirs

- The photographer's or T-shirt vendor's phone number for alumni wishing to purchase T-shirts. Alumni should be able to contact the company directly.

- Camera (for additional candid shots for the photo and/or memory album).

Chapter 11

After the Reunion

Congratulations, you successfully produced a milestone event! Except for a few loose ends, you can officially consider this masterful job, done.

CLOSING COSTS AND RESPONSIBILITIES

The only financial liability remaining should be the final payment to the photographer for the preparation and mailing of the photo albums. Payment will probably be required at the time you send in the paste up (described below) of the photo album.

The Photo Album

The photo album can be organized with the help of two persons in just a few hours. Try not to put off this project for very long; alumni will appreciate receiving it relatively soon after the reunion.

The photographer will send the reunion picture proofs along with the guests' names and addresses. He will provide instructions on completing the photo book. The following procedures will likely be required:

1. Verify that the alumni names correspond to their pictures and are spelled correctly.
2. Prepare an alphabetized list of names and addresses of all guests. This list will appear in the directory section of the photo album.

Print the attendance list with the names and addresses of alumni and their guests along with any additional alumni you want included in the photo album.

Suggestion: *Include all alumni that you have current addresses for.*

3. Design an introductory page with some brief statements. Here are some suggestions:

- Reunion facts: date, place and class reunion anniversary
- A picture of the high school or class insignia
- A list of award winners such as *"Who Came the Farthest to the Reunion?"*
- Names of committee members
- Statement from the committee about the reunion
- Memorial page
- A committee member's address and phone number to send address changes

Some of these items may already appear in your memory album, however, if you are combining a photo book with a memory album refer to additional suggestions described in Chapter 5 for designing a memory album.

4. Consolidate any pictures taken at the reunion and picnic and create one or more collage pages.

Thank You Notes

Thank you notes should be sent to special guests, the reunion coordinator of the high school, committee members who volunteered their time, those who donated their services or prizes and any other deserving people.

Memory Albums and Photo Books

Send memory albums and/or photo books to those alumni who paid for them. In addition, send albums to those alumni who paid for tickets, but were unable to attend the reunion.

The Bank Account

The reunion bank account should be closed after all bills have been paid and checks have cleared. If you budgeted carefully, there should be a balance remaining. Save it for the next reunion or divide the balance among the key people on the committee. A nice donation or gift to the high school in honor of your class reunion would also be a welcomed and thoughtful gesture.

Storage of Supplies

Get a box large enough to store any remaining memory albums, photo books, name tags, memorabilia and other reunion supplies. These supplies will be very helpful in planning the next reunion.

Put your reunion program
and files in a safe place.
Contact the publisher for
program updates.

CONCLUDING COMMENTS

In the next few weeks, while everything is still fresh in
your mind, write down your thoughts about the reunion such
as: "What would you do differently?" and "How would you
improve upon the next reunion?" These notes will be very
helpful when planning the next reunion.

The Post Reunion Blues

If you suffer from *post reunion let down,* consider doing a
follow up project like a newsletter. This will keep the
nostalgic ambiance alive, keep alumni informed and maintain
contact.

> Tulsa Central High School in Tulsa, Oklahoma puts out a regular
> newsletter to graduates of classes as far back as 1934. It offers newsy
> items about the high school, raises funds for a Foundation set up for
> the school, keeps alumni updated on upcoming reunions and
> maintains address records of the alumni.

On a personal note, I was able to preserve the nostalgic
glow by writing this book and helping with the development
of the computer program. With such projects in tow, I have
made many new friends and broadened my professional life.

Tell Us About Your Reunion

Please take a few moments to complete the Reunion
Survey on page 125. We would like to hear about your
reunion and include your ideas and anecdotes in our next
edition of *The Reunion Planner.*

POSTSCRIPT

Meeting a Challenge in Locating People   121
Survey   125

Meeting a Challenge in Locating People

I must confess, the most satisfying experience I encountered while writing this book involved unraveling a mystery I first thought would take too much effort and had a high degree of unresolvability. However, I became convinced that passivity or inaction should not be a response to challenges I may face. Here is my story:

In choosing a cover design for this book, my partner, Neal Barnett, and I selected one we thought was attractive and would emit a nostalgic glow. We thought any vintage school yearbook picture could portray the glimmer of those wonderful care-free years. Procuring such a picture was not as simple as we believed. We discovered that to display anyone's picture on the cover of a book, you must obtain that person's permission.

After contacting several image banks or stock houses, companies that sell pictures and illustrations, we learned that these companies mostly carry current photographs without the required release signatures (illustrations did not have the same feeling we wanted), and their dated photographs were too old.

The next idea was to use a picture from my own high school yearbook. "The pictures have the right feeling and you know the people," said Neal and Mark, the graphic designer. A cheerleading picture from my senior year was suggested and seemed to be the best choice, but I would have to locate and get the permission of all my former cheerleading squad members.

"Impossible" I said. "I haven't seen or heard from half of the group of eight for twenty-five years, or know if they're still alive. Furthermore, four of them were in a different class. Even if I find them, I don't know if they will want their picture on the cover of my book."

"You can find them," Neal insisted. "You offer many recommendations for locating people, follow your own advice."

"You're right, of course," I responded, and proceeded to undertake the mission.

Of the seven members in our squad I needed to find, three were in my class graduation year and had attended our twenty-year reunion. Two of the three, however, had moved with no forwarding address. The one person who hadn't moved, Phil, quickly and enthusiastically gave me his permission. Telephone information revealed that one of the squad members who moved, Evie, just relocated a few miles away in her same community. Fortunately, her husband was listed in the phone directory. She also was happy to help. The other woman who moved, Ann, was an attorney. I heard that the State Bar Association has the location of any attorney, so I called the Association and learned that Ann had moved to Washington D.C. Her response also was positive and encouraging.

With three former cheerleaders found, that left four to locate who graduated in a different year than I did.

A friend and former high school alum knew that one of these former cheerleaders, Gary, lived in a vicinity near her and she volunteered to call him and relay my request. I learned that Gary, too, was pleased to help and quickly provided his release signature. He also knew the whereabouts of Cathy, another member of our group. After a wonderful conversation with Cathy, that was complemented with happy recollections, she told me she thought that the parents of Nancy, another member of our group, still lived in the same house near the school. Telephone information revealed that, indeed, Nancy's family was still there and I got her phone number. After a spirited chat with Nancy, I concluded that even if I couldn't locate everyone, this experience had turned out to have a special significance in my life. I thoroughly enjoyed reconnecting with my cheerleading cohorts and catching up on their lives. The distance of time had disappeared.

Six found, one remaining, but no one had any idea where Tom was. He had a common name. I called all the same named people in the surrounding communities that were listed in the phone directory. We even recruited Neal's mother who tried calling all the people of the same name that were listed in even more nearby vicinities, to no avail. It didn't look promising. I couldn't use the picture if I was not able to find and get everyone's permission who posed in that photo twenty-five years ago.

Then, as I was meeting with our twenty-five year reunion committee, I mentioned that I was trying to locate Tom. One man recounted that his parents and Tom's were good friends and he knew Tom was practicing law in the county south of ours. Again, the California State Bar Association came through with his telephone number. I had found them all! Fortunately, Tom was also doing well and was enthusiastic about my endeavor. He even suggested that all of us get together and take a picture as we are today to include in the book.

"That's a great idea," I said. "Getting everyone together would be fun, and the picture a very special and unique accomplishment." Unfortunately, my printing deadline prohibits organizing such a reunion so quickly. However, for my next challenge . . .

Survey

Please take a moment to complete this survey, (even if only some questions are answered, we would appreciate your response). Tell us about some of your reunion experiences, whether organized by alumni or professional planners.

Who organized your reunion? (Alumni or professional planners?)

_____

Type of reunion _____
                         (High school, college, military etc.)
Place held _____
            (Hotel, restaurant, gym)
Date of reunion _____

Class size _____

Number of attendees (including guests) _____

How did you locate alumni?

_____

_____

Methods of contact _____

Did you contact alumni who were reluctant to attend? If so, did they change their minds? If so, why? _____
_____

What was your ticket price? _____

If tickets were mailed in advance, how soon before the reunion?
_____

Was the reception process well organized?
_____

What displays and/or decorations did you have?
_____
_____

What games, raffles or activities were offered? Were any special guests or former teachers invited?
_____
_____

What type of entertainment was provided? What did you like or dislike about it?
_____
_____

Was there a printed program? Awards? Door prizes?
_____
_____

What souvenirs were provided? e.g. Memory album, photo book, button name tags, etc.?
_____
_____

What items were available to purchase?
_____
_____

What did you like the most about your reunion?
_____
_____

What did you like the least?

_____

_____

Will you plan your next reunion? If not, why not?

_____

_____

_____

Do you have any interesting stories or anecdotes you would like to share?
They could be used in the next edition of our reunion guidebook.

_____

_____

_____

_____

School or organization name. (optional)

_____

ADDITIONAL COMMENTS

APPENDICES

A	Sample Invitations	131
B	Sample Questionnaire/Survey	135
C	Sample Accounting Ledgers	137
	Bibliography	141
	Index	143

ANNOUNCING
Point Loma High School
Class of 1973
Twenty Year Reunion

July 10, 1992

Dear Alumni:

Yes, it really is 20 years since we graduated and, yes, a reunion is being planned for next Fall, 1993.

We need your help! We're trying to locate all our fellow classmates and would like any assistance you can offer. Please refer to the enclosed "Missing Persons" list. Do you have any addresses, phone numbers or contacts for any classmates on this list? Also, we could use a few hours of your time with phoning or mailing.

Please complete the attached questionnaire to help us plan a reunion to your liking and give us an indication of how you can help.

A pot luck B-B-Q fund raiser, limited to 75 people, is planned for Labor Day, September 7, 1992 to help pay for hotel and entertainment deposits and other initial reunion expenses. Here are the details:

Monday, September 7, 1992
Home of Laura Rodgers
1150 Point Loma Blvd.
San Diego   *** BRING YOUR FAVORITE DISH ***
Cost: $15.00
Time: 12:30 - 5:00 p.m.

Your Reunion Committee,

Sally Bowman   Send your check to:
Sam Dunn   Point Loma Reunion Committee
Laura Rodgers   c/o Jeff Springer
Jeff Springer   1120 Cliff Drive
Pat Vazzana   San Diego, CA 92101

Washington High School
Class of 1967
25 Year Reunion

WHEN: *Saturday, September 19, 1992*

WHERE: *Canoga Park Hilton*
             15000 Canoga Avenue, Canoga Park

TIME: Social Hour: 6:30 p.m.
             Dinner: 8:00 p.m.

COST: *$50.00 per person BEFORE May 1, 1992*
             $55.00 per person May 1, 1992 and AFTER

PICNIC: *Westwood Park, Sunday, September 20, 1992*
             10844 Whitsett, Canoga Park

HOTEL Accommodations have been arranged for our group at a rate
of $85.00 per room at the Canoga Park Hilton. Mention our reunion
and make reservations by calling the hotel at (800)999-7000.

You will be missed if you do not plan on attending, but please complete
and send in the form below to help us keep our address list current.

· ·

Name_____Name of Guest_____
    Last   Maiden   First
Address_____Hm Phone(__)_____
         Street
_____Bus Phone(__)_____
  City,   State,   Zip

**Tickets will be mailed approximately 2 weeks before the reunion.
An acknowledgement will be sent upon receipt of your check.**

____I will not be able to attend the reunion, but please send me the
Reunion Memory Album at $10.00 each.

____Include my enclosed business card for listing in the Business
Directory @ $10.00 per card.

I am enclosing $_____
Make checks payable to Washington H S Reunion Committee
c/o Shelley (Lange) Jones
10080 Adams Blvd. Calabasas, CA 91302
For more information, call Shelley at (818)782-4321-H, (310)820-9999-B

Can you donate a door prize. If so, what _____

____I would be interested in purchasing a video of the reunion. The cost is estimated at $25.00.

Parent's or person's address and phone number who will always know your whereabouts._____
_____
_____

Please tell us what has transpired in your life since high school. This will be placed in a Memory Album to be distributed at the reunion. Or, recount one of your most memorable moments from high school that you would like to see in the Memory Album.

Please Attend...

Palisades High School
Class of 1979
Ten Year Reunion
on Saturday evening
the Fifth of August
Nineteen Hundred and Eighty—Nine
at the Beverly Wilshire Hotel
Starlight Ballroom
8950 Wilshire Blvd.
Beverly Hills, California
Check in, Cocktails — 6:30 p.m.
Dinner — 8:00 p.m.   Dancing — 'til 1:00 a.m.

Reunion Price

The cost for the evening will be $50 per Person/$95 per Couple. This will include the Memory Book which will be delivered to you approximately ten weeks after the reunion. No Host Bar. Dress Attire: Semi—Formal.

R.S.V.P.

Please respond by July 20, 1989. Enclose a check payable to "Palisades Class of '79 Committee" along with the tear—off below. Please fill out and return the attached questionnaire, too!

Hotel Accommodations

On Saturday night, rooms are available at the special rate of $120. Make your hotel reservations by calling (800) 999—4321.

— Tickets will be held at the door; your cancelled check is your receipt
— To keep our list current, please return the tear—off even if you do not plan to attend the event. Thank you.

Contacts: Bill Stevens (213) 555—3043   Bob Silvers (818) 555—2398

Name _____ Guest _____
    First   Maiden   Last

Address _____

City, St, Zip_____

Home Phone_____   Send to "Palisades Class of '79 Committee"
    2419 Sunset Blvd.

Work Phone _____   Pacific Palisades, CA 90049

Number Attending_____ Amount Enclosed $_____

Questionnaire

Name_____ Maiden Name _____

Spouse's Name_____

If married, how long?_____ No. of Children _____ Grandchildren_____

Pregnancy due date_____

Occupation _____

Hobbies/Interests_____

Did you marry your high school sweetheart?_____

What distance will you travel to attend the reunion?_____

How far do you live from the high school?_____

How many times have you moved since high school?_____

What classmates would you most like to see at the reunion?_____
_____

What former teachers would you like to invite to the reunion? _____
_____

Favorite song of our era._____

What was your most memorable event from high school?
_____
_____
_____
_____

Can you help in any way on the reunion committee?_____

Would you like to contribute to a donation being made to our school in honor of our class? If so, please include your donation along with your reservation/information form. Amount of donation $_____

We are accepting donations of non-perishable food items to be given to (the charity of your choice).

Please send in a current picture of yourself and your family for display at our reunion or if you cannot attend the reunion, for our memory album.

Survey

The results of this anonymous survey will be available at the reunion or mailed to you upon request. Just check off the appropriate answer and return in the enclosed envelope.

<hr>

_____   _____   _____   _____
Male/Female   Married?   No. Children   State Residing In

My current position on the following issues and topics:

Issue/Topic	For	Against
U.S. President		
Term Limits for Congress		
Legalizing Abortion		
Death Penalty		
Affirmative Action		
Legalizing Drugs		
National Health Care		
Smoking in Public Facilities		
Dress Codes in Schools		
Year Round School		
School Busing		
Sex Education in Schools		
Higher Taxes for Education		
More Police Presence in Neighborhoods		

Sample Accounting Ledger

Receipts

Last Name (Maiden)	First	No. Attg	Item Purch	Amt Paid	Running Total
(Gordon) Jones	Laura	2	tkts	$100	$100
Zack	Alan	1	tkt	50	150
Vazzana	Pat	1	tkt	50	200
Henderson	Sam	0	book	10	210
(Sloan) Jacobs	Teri	2	tkts	100	310
Davis	Tim	2	tkts	100	410
Johansen	Ed	1	tkt	50	460
March Total		**9**		**$460**	**$460**

Last Name (Maiden)	First	No. Attg	Item Purch	Amt Paid	Running Total
Geis	Brian	0	book	$10	$470
Jackson	Scott	2	tkts	100	570
Little	Mike	1	tkt	50	620
(Lennon) Bair	Shari	2	tkts	100	720
(Post) Silver	Susan	1	tkt	50	770
(Klein) Baker	Bev	0	2 books	20	790
Wilder	John	2	tkts	100	890
April/May Total		**8**		**$430**	**$890**

Page Total   **17**   **$890**

Expenses

Description	Unit Cost	# of Units	Cost	Running Total
Rubber Stamp	$16.00		$16.00	$16.00
Printing (1st Mailer)	24.95		24.95	40.95
Envelopes	7.00		7.00	47.95
Postage (1st Mailer)	0.29	500	145.00	192.95
Deposit on Ballroom	1,000.00		1,000.00	1,192.95
Entertainment Dep.	300.00		300.00	1,492.95
Park Reservation	35.00		35.00	1,527.95
Monthly bank fee	3.00		3.00	1,530.95
Banner	107.50		107.50	1,638.45
Name Tags	0.50	250	125.00	1,763.45
Printing (2nd Mailer)	20.95		20.95	1,784.40
Ackmnt Postcards	0.29	100	29.00	1,813.40
Monthly bank fee	3.00		3.00	1,816.40

As of July 31st

Total Revenues to date: $2,445.00
Total Expenses to date: 1,816.40
Balance: $ 628.60
Check book balance: $ 628.60

© WILSON JONES COMPANY G7208 GREEN 7208 BUFF Accounting Ledger

	Last Name (Maiden)	Married	First Name	Number Attending	Item Purchased	Amount Paid	Running Total
	1	2	3	4	5	6	7
1							
2							
3							
4							
5							
6							
7							
8							
9							
10							
11							
12							
13							
14	Total For: (Period)						
15							

Accounting Ledger
Ticket Purchases

Date	Last Name (Maiden)	Last Name Married	First	Amount Paid	Running Total
1					
2					
3					
4					

COLUMN WRITE ®

Accounting Ledger
Advertising Purchases

Date	Last Name (Maiden)	Last Name Married	First	Amount Paid	Running Total
1					
2					
3					
4					
5					

COLUMN WRITE ®

Bibliography

Hammond, Robert A. "...So Get it on Videotape and have the Last Laugh." *Popular Photography* (June 1988): 58-59. Subtitled "Planning to attend your class reunion or (even better) someone else's? Let your camcorder and videotape bring home the memories." A complete description on how to videotape your reunion. It includes many ideas and recommendations for recording a reunion event.

Lamb, Douglas H., and Reeder, Glenn D. "Reliving Golden Days." *Psychology Today* (June 1986): 22-30. Subtitled "Yes, You Can Relive Those Thrilling Days of Yesteryear, and The Older You Are The More Likely You Are To Enjoy It." This article summarizes the findings from the authors research on attendees of a five-day reunion event for anyone who ever graduated from a school in a middle-class community on the East Coast.

Markey, Judy. *How to Survive Your High School Reunion...and Other Mid-life Crises.* Chicago: Contemporary Books, 1984. A funny and thoughtful book about how to deal with entering middle age. The first part of her book includes an 11 point advisory program recommending steps to take in order to enjoy one's high school reunion.

Ninkovich, Tom. *Reunion Handbook: For School and Military Reunions. 2nd ed.,* San Francisco: Reunion Research, 1989. A reunion guidebook with a section on military reunions. Also has a helpful resource guide for trivia facts, graphics supplies and designing newsletters.

Poli, Kenneth. "Critical Focus." *Popular Photography* (September 1984): 20-22. Subtitled "Nostalgia isn't what it used to be? Don't you believe it! Photos make it better than ever." An article describing in detail about how the author made all the photo button name tags for his reunion.

Reunions, The Magazine. A quarterly magazine that has articles, stories, how-tos, advertisements, announcements about reunion services, products and ways to connect with other reunion planners. It addresses all types of organizations that hold reunions including family, club, religious groups and schools. The magazine is based in Milwaukee, Wisconsin. If you would like further information or want to subscribe to the magazine, they can be reached by calling (414)263-4567.

Silver, Susan. *Organized to be the Best!: Winning Solutions to Simplify How You Work.* Los Angeles: Adams-Hall, 1989. An excellent book with many ideas and tips to organize your personal and professional life.

Worthington, Daniel L. *Isn't it Time For a Reunion? 7th ed.,* Santa Ana: Worthington Reunion Photographers, 1992. This succinct booklet is another useful tool that describes how to plan your reunion. In the reunion business for many years, the author not only provides the photography for reunions, including a full color memory album, he also offers many other services such as locating classmates, making name tags and selling engraved souvenirs.

Index

Accounting guidelines, 77,
App. C
Acknowledgement postcards, 77
78p
Acknowledgements
for donations, 93
as payment receipts, 59, 77
Address Correction Requested,
58
Address labels, 62, 75
Advertising income, 42, 67
Agenda, for program, 91-94,
92p
Announcements, 93
during program, 91, 93, 113
as invitations, 58, 73,
media, 81
to school, 18
Attendance list, 97, 101,
Awards, 93, 94, 98

Balloons, 81-82
Bank account
closing of, 117
opening of, 68
Banners, 83, 83p
Before leaving the event, 113
Budget, Chap. 2, 37p, 38p
advertising income, 42

assumptions, 36
balancing of, 43
bank account, 68, 115
computer program, 44
estimated balance, 43
estimated expenses, 39-41
estimated revenues, 41-42
raising additional cash, 43-44
seed money, 24
Button name tags, 71, Biblio.

Camps, conference centers,
lodges, 30
Cash box, 103, 104, 113
Centerpieces, 81-83, 82p
Checklist, Reunion, 31-34
Class reunion committees of
earlier years, 23
Closing costs, 115
Committees, 18-24
final meeting, 101
first meeting, 18-21
need for organizing, 21
registration meeting, 101
responsibilities, 19
second mailing, 73
setting up of, 20
Computer program, 8, 9-11, 9p
address labels, 57, 75, 99

Computer program *(continued)*
  attendance list, 98
  budget, 35, 44
  database for survey, 61
  entering alumni list, 16
  missing alumni, 74
  phone lists, 21, 80
  printing features, 10
    name tags, 72, 90
    paid list, 90, 98, 116
    payments, 78
    reunion invitations, 58,
      App. A,
    storage of files, 118
    ticket payments, 78
    updating data, 23
Contingency plan, 106
Correspondence
  as inducements to attend, 47
County Assessor, 23
County Hall of Records, 23
County Marriage License
  Bureaus, 23
County Registrar of Voters, 23
Coupons, for donations, 94, 94p

Decisions
  to plan reunion, 7-8
  when and where to have the
    reunion, 24
Decorations, 81-85
  balloons, 81-82
  banner, 83
  centerpieces, 81-83, 82p
  "In Memorial" display, 85
  napkins, 84
  nostalgia table, 84
  picture blowups, 84

  picture collage, 85
  setting up, 94
  signs, 95
  as themes, 25, 82
  wine bottle, inscribed, 83
Dept of Motor Vehicles, 23
Disc jockey, 63
  as master of ceremonies, 92
Door prizes, 94
  donations of, 61, 91
  during program, 93-94, 113

Encouraging attendance
  Chap. 3
Entertainment, 63-66
  activities and games, 64
  hiring supplemental
    performers, 49
  as inducement to attend, 49
  musical accompaniment, 63
  slide show, 65-66
  video tape, 65
  where to find, 63
Estimated balance, 43
Estimated expenses, 39-41
Estimated revenues, 41-42
Event, The Reunion, Chap. 10

Files, 68
Finding alumni, 20-23
  alumni referrals, 59, 80
  begin the search, 21
  correspondence, 58
  media ads, 81
  missing persons lists, 23, 62,
    74
  phone drive, 79
  school as liaison, 16-18, 18p

Finding alumni *(continued)*
  school lists, 16
First committee meeting, 20-24
  first mailing, 57-63
  search for alumni, 20
  seed money, 24
Fund raisers, 24, 43

Groundwork, Chap. 1

High school
  contacts, 16-18
  place for reunion, 29, 68
Hotels, 25, 28
  flyer inside mailer, 75

Information sheet, 59-61,
  App. B
Initial funding (see seed
  money)
Insignia, class, 70, 70p
Introduction, 1-12
  of special guests, 91, 113
Invitation samples, App. A, 58,
  73, 93

Jukebox, 63

Last-minute items
  cash needs, 44, 100
  details, 101, 106
  reservations, 77, 97, 98
Letters
  from classmates, 84
  registration table, 103, 103p
Loose ends, 98-99

Mailing labels, 61, 62, 75, 99
Mailings
  acknowledgements, 78

first mailing, 57-63
to increase attendance, 47
reminder notices, 89
second mailing, 73-75
tickets, 99
Mansions/Estates/Museums, 29
Marriage License Bureau, 23
Master of Ceremonies, 63, 92
Meal count, 105
Media ads, 81
Meetings
  final meeting, 101
  first meeting, 20-24
    collect seed money, 24
    search for alumni, 20-24
  mailing meetings, 57-63, 73-75
Mementos, 81, 83, 84
Memorabilia, 84
Memorials, 71, 85, 116
Memory album, 69-71, 98
Missing persons list, 62, 74
Movie posters, 84
Musical accompaniment, 63
  volume control, 64

Name tags, 71-73, 102, 72p
  computer generated, 72
  making the tags, 89
Napkins, 85
Necessities, Reunion Day, 110
Newsletters, 118
Newspapers (see media ads)
No-shows, 105
Nostalgia table, 84

Overview of this book, 12

Phone drive, 48, 79-81, 89
Photo album, 115-17
Photographer, 66, 112, 114

Photographer cards, 96, 102
Picnic, 6, 67-68, 113-14
Picture blowups, 84
Picture collage, 85, 133
Places to hold reunions, 28-30
Post reunion blues, 118
Postage, 39-40, 62, 75
Postcards
  acknowledgements, 78, 78p
  reminder notices, 89, 90p
Pre-paid ticket holders, 104
Presentations, 91, 93, 113
Professional reunion planners,
  4-7, 44
  contract with, 6
Program, 90-94, 113
  printed, 90-91, 91p
  spoken, 91-94
  updates, 98
Pros and Cons of planning a
  reunion, 3, 3p

Questionnaires, App. B
  computer database, 61
  in invitations, 60, 73
Questions for the Catering
  Manager, 26-27

Radio ads, 81
Raffle, 43
Raising additional cash, 43-44
Reception desk, 85p
  items, 103
  responsibilities, 104
  will call table, 102, 104
  workers, 85-86, 98, 112
Refunds, 105
Registration, 85p, 101-04
  contents of packets, 102
  packet inscription, 102p

Reluctant reunion attendees
  dealing with, 50-55
Reminder notices, 89, 90p
Reservation form, 59, App. A
Response envelope, 61, 75
Reunion announcements and
  invitation samples, App. A
Reunion committee, 18-22
  final/registration meeting, 101
  first meeting, 18-21
  need for organizing, 21
  responsibilities, 19
  search for alumni, 20
  second mailing meeting, 73
  setting up of, 18
Reunion Day Necessities, 109,
  110p
Reunion Event, The, Chap. 10
Rubber stamp, 62

School as contact, 15-18
Search for alumni, 20
Second mailing, 73-75
Seed money, 24
Set up
  bank account, 68
  banquet room, 109
  decorations, 95
Signs, 95, 103
Slide show, 65-66, 99
Special events, 64
Special guests, 49, 98
  introduction of, 113
Storage of supplies, 117
Structure of book, 11-12
  The Countdown, 87
  The Footwork, 45
  Getting Organized, 13
  Reunion Day and Afterwards,
  107

Survey, 125-28, 134
 in mailers, 60
 in memory album, 71

Tape deck, 63
Telephone books, 22
Thank you notes, 117
Tickets, 76-77, 76p
 accounting guidelines, 77
 inside registration packets,
   102
 mailing, 99
T-shirts, 84, 98, 114

Video tape, 65, Biblio.

Weekend combination of
 events, 30
Will call table, 102, 104
Wine bottle inscription, 83

Yacht cruise, 28
Yearbooks
 bring to reunion, 66
 for name tags, 71

App.   = Referenced within Appendix
Biblio. = Referenced within Bibliography
p   = Picture or figure

The Reunion Planner™ Computer Program

The optional computer program designed to be used with this book, has everything you need to simplify and streamline your reunion plan.

- Sort, Browse, and Print Alumni Lists
- Calculate and Monitor a Budget
- Design and Print Your Own Invitations and Flyers
- Print Address Labels
- Print Phone Lists
- Print Name Tags
- Print Task Checklists
- And Much More!

Why not order additional copies of
The Reunion Planner
for other committee members or friends?

- -

To order, complete this form and send your check to:

Goodman Lauren Publishing, 11661 San Vicente Blvd. Suite 505, Dept. B, Los Angeles, CA 90049

Please send me The Reunion Planner Computer Program
I prefer   5 1/4" ☐   3 1/2" ☐   Diskette
Requirements: IBM Compatible, DOS 3.0+, 640K, Hard Disk

Name:_____

Address:_____

City:_____State:_____Zip:_____

Phone: _____

Computer Program	Qty:_____ x $ 42.95 =	$_____
Additional Books	Qty:_____ x $ 12.95 =	_____
Program/Book Combos	Qty:_____ x $ 45.95 =	_____

California Residents, Add 8.25% Sales Tax: _____

Shipping & Handling — $2.50 (+.75/ea add'l item): _____

TOTAL:$_____